Learning While Black

LARRY P. REVISITED

IQ Testing of African Americans

SECOND EDITION

William Thomas

NEWMAN SPRINGS PUBLISHING
320 Broad Street
Red Bank, NJ 07701

First originally published by Newman Springs Publishing 2019

ISBN 978-1-64531-758-6 (Paperback)
ISBN 978-1-64531-759-3 (Digital)

Printed in the United States of America

Proceedings of a symposium presented by the Department of African American Studies of City College of San Francisco and the Bay Area Association of Black Psychologists on February 25, 1998.

Edited by William A. Thomas
Larry P. Revisited: IQ Testing of African Americans

CONTENTS

ACKNOWLEDGMENTS

Acknowledgment and appreciation are expressed to the many people who helped make the symposium a success because of their many generous contributions. These include the City College of San Francisco Staff Development Office and the Bay Area Association of Black Psychologists for their financial support; campus faculty and staff who helped with innumerable tasks from moderators and recorders to publicity, duplication, and audio-visual services; Edie Burnett who managed registration; Ann-Paige Ewing who was hospitality chair; Alma Maxwell who transported visitors to and from the airport and campus; and most importantly, symposium participants who critically but warmly helped us and each other.

A strong support system is what enabled me to persevere while writing this book. For example, my faith and spirituality gave me a hopeful outlook on life, and kept me humble. Included also were the following: my wife Yvonne's generosity and encouragement; the un-selfish affection of my children and grandchildren; brother Arthur and wife Virginia whose home is where no one is made to feel like a stranger; cousins Artha Juntunen, Betty RiChard, and Juliet Cochran who are good listeners whenever I need to talk; psychiatrist John Straznickas, life coach, and sagacious friend at the San Francisco Veterans Administration; Nkechi Townsend, a fellow Elder and warrior for justice in the Association of Black Psychologists; professional colleagues Lawford and Marilyn Goddard, and Anita Gilbert whose knowledge of ethics in the field of psychology is admirable; last, but not least, Robert Wilson, my wife's eldest son, a computer wizard who gives freely of his time and expertise.

INTRODUCTION

On February 25,1998, a historic gathering occurred on the campus at City College of San Francisco. Nearly three hundred psychologists, psychiatrists, lawyers, students, mental health workers, and community activists convened for a symposium on IQ Testing of African Americans. The symposium, as participants and several observers reported, was a rousing success. Co-sponsors of this event were the African American Studies department at City College of San Francisco and the Bay Area Association of Black Psychologists. Coordinators William Thomas, Veronica Hunnicutt, Glenn Nance, and the more than two hundred other activist-intellectuals who joined them in planning the symposium viewed it as the launching of a renewed struggle against the misuse of IQ tests with African Americans.

The symposium was organized at a critical moment in time. Judicial, legislative, and racial terrorist attacks have accelerated since the early 1990s. African Americans and the programs undergirding their scant improvements since the civil rights movement are increasingly under attack. Legislative bodies in several states and in Washington, DC, are poised to join California in outlawing Affirmative Action programs. The Special Education Department in the state of California has established a committee to explore ways to circumvent the Larry P. decision. Racially motivated hate crimes are increasing in number and in seriousness, examples are the random killing of Ricky Byrdsong by Benjamin Nathniel Smith in Chicago, Illinois; the police torture of Haitian immigrant Abner Louima and the execution with forty-one bullets of Guinean immigrant Amadou Diallo in New York City; the murder of black teenager Tyisha Miller by the police in Riverside, California; and the dragging death of James Byrd Jr. in Jasper, Texas.

In 1954, the United States Supreme Court decided in Brown v. the Topeka, Kansas Board of Education that separate but equal education is inherently unequal. This decision overturned the 1896 Plessy v. Ferguson separate but equal law.

It was out of this legacy of American history that it became necessary to promulgate laws of racial and cultural inclusion.

The Treaty of Guadalupe Hidalgo guaranteed Mexican Americans protection of their culture and language. It is quite interesting that this protection was never actually implemented, and thousands of Latin American people to this day are placed in educable mentally retarded classes because of linguistic and/or cultural differences diagnosed, for the most part, with inappropriate standardized tests.

For the generation of the civil rights movement of the 1960s and 1970s, it was generally recognized that the time had come to remove barriers of segregation and establish a truly egalitarian nation. New laws were added by the courts and new legislation by Congress to insure that members of a lower economic class or races and cultures which have suffered most severely from the ravages of social exclusion would now have the chance to participate equally. However, with the continued administration of IQ tests, black and other ethnically diverse students are held to standards which are racially and culturally discriminatory to them even if integrated schools provide them the opportunity to participate equally.

Standardized testing—history's short memory? For the generation of the 60s and 70s, it was quite clear to most people what the civil rights movement was all about. It was generally recognized that certain groups of people had been excluded from participating equally in the everyday life of this society because of their race and culture. The time had come, it was thought, to remove these barriers of exclusion and establish a truly egalitarian nation. Out of this belief grew the concept of affirmative action or the idea that this country could live up to the liberal tradition upon which it was founded, if all of its sons and daughters were given equal opportunities of access.

Those who believed this also understood that the long history of exclusion had created unequal circumstances for these people, especially for those who had suffered the most. It was expected that it might take a little more time for those who had been held down longest and treated more harshly to arrive at a level of inclusion which many took for granted as a God-given right.

Today we hear strange voices of all political stripes crying for a "level playing field" and the elimination of privilege or preferential treatment for some, i.e., Proposition 209 in California. It would appear that the cry was intended for students or parents of groups, races or cultures which have suffered from the not too distant ravages of social exclusion that they would now have the chance to participate equally. This sounds very egalitarian, at least on the surface. The idea that no one should receive special privileges or preferential treatment of any sort does, at first glance, seem to guarantee equality for all. However, for those who are still suffering from the effects of past exclusion and haven't been able to partake in the privileges that many take for granted, the term *equality* has no meaning. How could anyone have equal opportunity today if they are still suffering from the ravaging effects of unequal treatment of the past? Even if they had the opportunity to participate equally, they would be held to standards which are racially and culturally discriminatory to them. Until adequate measuring instruments can be devised for the contextual assessment of academic achievement which would take into consideration the uniqueness of all students, the further use of tests such as the IQ and SAT will do more to damage the psyches of these students than measure their present-day capabilities or predict their future success.

Historically, there is a rather extensive literature on ability and achievement testing in the schools that has been identified as a main source of bias for black school children (Thomas 1975). Barnes (1972) alleged that psychologists who administer traditional ability and achievement tests consistently assign false labels to black children, thereby contributing to their intellectual genocide; that is, they use biased test results to exclude black children from intellectual experiences that would prepare them for school and success in life.

Barnes contended that psychologists deny black children higher educational opportunities by using test results to establish educational tracking within which the majority of black children are assigned to lower education tracks.

Williams pointed out the abuses of tests as they are used by psychologists with black children, noting that "although black children comprise only 27.8 percent of the total student population in the San Francisco Unified Schools, they comprise 47.4 percent of all students in educational handicapped classes and 53.3 percent of all students in the educable mentally handicapped classes" (Williams 1971, 67).

The effects of the examiner on test scores has been identified as another source of bias, especially when the examiner is white and the student is black (Katz 1964, Barnes 1972, and Katz et al. 1964). It was found by Katz (1964) that when the administrator of an intellectual test is white and when comparison with white peers is anticipated, black subjects tend to become fearful of failure.

> Anticipation of failure elicits feelings of being victimized and overt hostility toward the tester. Because overt expression of hostility toward white authority is fraught with danger, the impulse is suppressed and elicits emotional responses disruptive to the subject's test performance. (Barnes 1972, 71)

In another experiment, Katz (1964) compared the effects of black and white examiners on the test performance of black pupils and concluded that the effect varied with the nature of the task. Better performance was elicited by white examiners when the task was not perceived as intellectual in nature. When the task was viewed as a measure of intelligence, performance was better with black examiners. Barnes (1972) reported similar findings. Psychologists who test and screen children for special education classes are usually white. Their ignorance of black history, language, psychology, and sociology could well constitute another source of bias.

Larry P. Revisited: I.Q. Testing of African Americans is primarily a series of papers selected from presenters at the 1998 City College Symposium. Additionally, two seminal articles by Asa Hilliard were culled from the literature, with permission of the publisher, to provide useful perspectives not stated elsewhere.

Larry P. is a pseudonym for one of the plaintiffs in a 1971 class action suit filed against Wilson Riles, Superintendent of Instruction for California, the California State Department of Education, and the San Francisco School Board over the placement of black children into classes for the educable mentally retarded (EMR).

Psychologists from the Association of Black Psychologists (ABPsi) reexamined 5 children who had been placed into EMR classes using the same IQ tests as had been used by San Francisco Unified School District psychologists. They found none of the children to be retarded. The case came to trial in 1977 and was decided in favor of the Plaintiff by Judge Robert Peckham in 1980. In San Francisco, Judge Robert Peckham ruled in favor of the Plaintiffs against the use of IQ tests.

Peckham, in his 1979 ruling, barred California public schools from using IQ tests for determining whether academically struggling Black students should be placed in special classes for the mildly mentally retarded, a decision which stands until today.

This revised edition of Larry P. Revisited: I.Q. Testing of African Americans has been divided into six chapters, and includes an epilogue, biographical sketches and an appendix.

Chapter one is centered on the history of IQ tests as a history of racial prejudice, social Darwinism and scientific mystic to legitimate such prejudice. Other chapters are related to legal issues and the Courts, racial and ethic bias in test construction, alternative methods for non-biased assessment, and implications for research and practice.

CHAPTER

1

They Still Don't Get It

Robert L. Williams

First, in the tradition of my African ancestry, permit me to call upon the Creator to be in our presence and to guide us here today and forever as we trod along life's paths. We must also call upon our ancestors upon whose shoulders we stand and in whose paths we walk. We must realize that our ancestors laid the foundation for human civilization; they provided the wisdom by which we live and the models by which our lives are guided. We call upon our elders whose children we are to provide the generational continuity so that our culture is transmitted from generation to generation.

To the present generation and to the unborn and future generations, we call upon the spirits of our children and our children's children to witness what we are doing.

Let us remember that we built great pyramids in Kemet, and they still remain. We call upon the spirits of our children and our children's children to witness what we are doing.

Let us remember that we built great pyramids in Kemet, and they still remain. We are also able to build great schools and institutions to provide world-class education.

Remember the ancestors. Remember the crossing. Remember the struggle. Remember the victory. ASHE.

I am extremely thankful to Dr. William Thomas for this invitation to speak at this conference. That was a warm introduction. I've got big shoes to fill from that. It's always good to see old friends. I've seen Harold Dent. I lived in San Francisco in 1968 and 1969 and worked for the National Institute of Mental Health. When Bill called and asked me to come, I had to ask him to change the date because February is a very busy month.

I'd like to begin in the tradition of our ancestors. It is important for us to recognize our ancestors on whose shoulders we stand. I want them to witness us today and our struggle. This struggle is a very personal one for me. It takes me back a number of years.

The continuing disputes over the intellectual inferiority of African Americans and the corresponding problem of measuring their intelligence have generated a tremendous amount of heat (and less light) over the past seventy-five years. Let me state my position at the outset as follows:

1. Black Americans are not intellectually, emotionally, spiritually, or psychologically inferior to white Americans.
2. The real issue is not whether black Americans are less intelligent than white Americans but rather the serious under educational achievement and miseducation of our African American children.

Personal story

Let me begin with how I became involved with the testing movement and its issues. Three events occurred in my life that set me on the path of criticizing the cultural bias in tests. One of the reasons that I became involved with the IQ test controversy is that I was virtually one of its casualties.

When I was in the tenth grade at Dunbar High School in Little Rock, I was given an IQ test. I tested out in the slow group because I earned a score of 82. My counselor told me I barely missed the mentally retarded classes by 3 IQ points. But when she told me my score, I smiled thinking that an 82 was at least a *B* or a *B* minus.

But the counselor frowned and told me I couldn't go to college because, "You do not have the ability to go to college." She enrolled me in a vocational trade curriculum. As a consequence in high school, I took auto mechanics, bricklaying, electricity, and carpentry—the usual vocational trade courses. I did slip into some English, math, and science courses.

The reason I went to college was that I was working as a waiter one night when a fellow was working an algebra problem, and I saw that he was making an error. I said, "Chester, you're not doing the problem right." I showed him how to work the problem.

He said, "If you can work this problem and these problems on this page, then you should be in college."

I couldn't wait. I went to junior college for a year. After a two-year hiatus, I went on to Philander Smith College, and I graduated with honors in the top five of my class, cum laude, laudy, laudy, and thank you, laudy.

It didn't stop there.

I left down south and went to Wayne State University in Detroit (up south) because in those days, blacks were not allowed to enroll in allwhite graduate programs in the South. It was there at Wayne State that I did my first piece of research on the IQ test. My master's thesis investigated the comparison of traditional versus culturally fair IQ tests on fourth grade black and white children. I administered the Davis-Eels games, cultural fair test, and the Henman-Nelson conventional test. The results were striking. Black children performed as well or better on the culturally-specific test than the white children. If you had a test that was culturally fair or culturally common then the children would do much better. That was the first event along with my IQ score in high school that really started me in the direction of working in this business of protesting and fighting the IQ testing industry—the master's thesis and my score of 82.

I enrolled in graduate school in September 1957 at Washington University, the year of the Little Rock Nine, and graduated in 1961 with a doctorate in clinical psychology—the first African American to do so in psychology at Washington University.

Unfortunately, my instructors at Washington University were not interested in the IQ testing issue. So I could not engage in the continuation of this important issue of pursuing bias in testing. Instead, my doctoral thesis was entitled, "An Investigation into the Relationship between Body Image and Physiological Response Pattern in Patients with Peptic Ulcer and Rheumatoid Arthritis." I am now a retired professor of psychology from Washington University, author of more than sixty articles and two books. I have been invited to speak at most of the major universities in this country. Not bad for a black man with an IQ of 82. My point is that there are numerous black children who are mislabeled or misplaced because of the racism in IQ testing.

The second event that sent me in this direction was the founding of the Association of Black Psychologists in 1968 in San Francisco. That's where I met Harold Dent, and we worked together for National Institute of Mental Health. Harold and I were consultants or insultants, I should say. We proposed seven concerns to the American Psychological Association. I became involved with the fourth item in the petition. We therefore proposed that the American Psychological Association will immediately establish a committee to study the misuse of standardized psychological instruments to maintain and justify the practice of systematically denying educational and economic opportunities to black youth. Further that pending, the thorough review and reassessment of the issue on the highly questionable validity of these measures, a moratorium be declared on comparative testing and evaluation projects (Williams 1974).

The response to ABPsi's petition of concerns was evasive and nonproductive. Dr. George Albee, then president of APA, reported the following to ABPsi: "With respect to the request of the Association of Black Psychologists, it is inappropriate for the board or council of the association to 'endorse' or to purport to speak for 30,000 members on any issue or issues" (Williams 1974).

It became increasingly clear that the APA did not intend to endorse, support, or respond to our seven petitions of concerns especially since it had vested interests in psychological tests. ABPsi decided to move independently of APA (Williams 1999).

As early as 1969 (thirty years ago), the Association of Black Psychologists called for a moratorium on testing African American children with IQ tests. The moratorium stated that the Association of Black Psychologists fully supports those parents who have chosen to defend their rights by refusing to allow their children and themselves to be subjected to achievement, intelligence, aptitude, and performance tests which are being used to:

1. label black children as uneducable;
2. place black children in special classes;
3. potentiate inferior education;
4. assign black children to lower educational tracks than whites;
5. deny black children higher educational opportunities; and
6. destroy positive intellectual growth and development of black children (Williams 1974).

The third event that sent me in the direction of fighting the testing industry was the development of the BITCH test. In 1968, I coined the phrase Black Intelligence Test for Honkies. That title, as you can imagine, created a firestorm of controversy. I received over two hundred letters of protest from Caucasian psychologists. Later, I changed the name to the Black Intelligence Test of Cultural Homogeneity.

The BITCH is a culturally specific test. It is not intended to be culturally fair or culturally common. The first problem is item selection. The test items were drawn exclusively from the black experience domain. The original word pool included four hundred items. All items were edited to eliminate careless phraseology, ambiguity, and misspellings. The items were administered to black and white subjects in order to identify (1) the criteria for defining the words and (2) the items common to black and white groups and items that pulled associations peculiar to white groups.

The next step involved tryout sessions with a group of four judges, two blacks and two whites, who rated the items for ambiguity, clarity, and objectivity. The tryout sessions proved helpful in de-emphasizing some items and sharpening others. Final item selection consisted of the best one hundred items from the original pool.

I developed this instrument to make a statement about the cultural bias in testing. The Black Intelligence Test showed startling results in 1969. Blacks were not low in IQ; whites were. Dr. Horace Mitchell, vice chancellor of Business Operations at the University of California, Berkeley, conducted his dissertation research using the Black Intelligence Test. The purpose of the study was to examine the relationship between white counselors' sensitivity to the black experience and their counseling effectiveness with black clients.

The author concludes, "The generally low level of counselor sensitivity to the black experience indicated a dire need of providing more experiences during training which are designed to increase the level of sensitivity to the black experience." The finding was that those white counselors who had personal or socially equal relationships with blacks had a tendency to be more sensitive. Those who had little or no experience with blacks were less sensitive, showed little empathy and were less sensitive.

How do you know where I'm at if you ain't been where I've been? Understand where I'm coming from? (*Good Times* 1974).

So I had three events that sent me in this direction: the IQ test of 82, the BITCH test, and the Association of Black Psychologists. With that background, I began to fight IQ testing.

Let us take a look at the word *intelligence*. First of all, intelligence is a construct. It is a hypothetical construct. It is a concept which attempts to explain phenomena which are presumed to exist in the individual. As a concept, there are many definitions of intelligence. There is not one definition. You always have to think of intelligence as a construct. In order to prove or define what is intelligence, it is operationally defined through an IQ test. IQ and intelligence are not synonymous. They are not interchangeable. That's an important point to know. A lot of the studies that come out will talk about IQ as if it is intelligence, and I submit to you they are not the same.

IQ is a measurement, presumably, of intelligence. IQ is the operational definition of intelligence, that is, it represents allegedly the measurement of intelligence by some method. Just as a tape or ruler accurately measures inches, feet, and yards or a scale accurately measures weight in pounds, an IQ is supposed to measure this thing called intelligence. But IQ tests do not have the same kind of scaling units as scales and rulers. There is no true zero point, and the intervals are not necessarily equal, i.e., an IQ of 150 is not twice an IQ of 75. Thus, when reports show that black Americans have lower IQs, this is not to be taken that we have lower intelligence. All it means is that blacks scored lower on the test than whites.

Thus the meaning of intelligence is rather diverse, and although considerable attention has been given this construct, it is still ill-used and poorly defined. Definitions of intelligence are so diverse that it would be impractical to list them here. Here are several that are representatives:

1. Intelligence is what the intelligence tests measure.
2. Intelligence is defined by a consensus among psychologists.
3. Intelligence is the repertoire of intellectual skills and knowledge available to a person at any one period of time (Humphreys 1971).
4. Intelligence is the summation of learning experiences of the individual (Wesman 1968).
5. Intelligence is the aggregate or global capacity of the individual to act purposefully, to think rationally, and to deal effectively with his environment (Wechsler 1958).

I would like to offer a different approach, one which I refer to as the *rubber band concept of intelligence*. My contention is that people are born with different genetic potentials just as there are different sizes of rubber bands—*small*, *medium*, and *large*. The genes set the extent to which the rubber band (intelligence) can be stretched. The environment develops the rubber band to its "stretch potential" or in many instances the environment hinders the stretch potential from being developed. Some persons live in environments that develop their potential whereas others live in environments that do not.

Early development of IQ tests

Historically, five Europeans have been responsible for the development of IQ tests in the USA—an Englishman, Sir Francis Gaitan; a German, William Stern; a Frenchman, Alfred Binet; and two Americans, Henry Goddard and Lewis Terman.

Gaitan initiated the ideas of measuring individual differences of abilities. He devised some of the first techniques of mental measurements (Gaitan 1869). Gaitan also introduced the term *eugenics* to the world. According to Gaitan, eugenics was the study of the agencies under social control that may improve or impair the racial qualities of future generations. Stated differently, eugenics is the science of the improvement of the human race through better breeding. Conceived as a scientifically grounded reform movement in an age of social and political turbulence, eugenics looked to hereditary factors for the source of a vast array of human problems such as feeblemindedness, criminality, rebelliousness, and alcoholism. Eugenicists also thought they had found the causes of many fundamental social problems in measurable defects.

In France, Alfred Binet was commissioned by the minister of Public Education in 1904 to develop instruments to determine students whose failure in school required some special education. In 1905, Binet developed the first scale which became the forerunner of the modern-day IQ test although he stated that his scale "does not permit the measure of intelligence." Binet insisted on three principles to be observed in the use of his tests. However, the American psychologists who translated his scales into English later disregarded all of his warnings.

Binet's warning were as follows:

1. The scores are a practical device; they do not support a theory of intellect. They do not measure anything innate and do not designate what they measure as intelligence.

2. The scale is a rough, empirical guide for identifying mildly retarded and learning disabled children who need special help.

3. Whatever the cause of the difficulty in children identified for help, emphasis should be placed on improvement rather than labeling.

If Binet's principles had been followed and his test consistently used as he developed them, we would not have the kind of misuse and mislabeling controversies that we have today. American psychologists perverted Binet's intentions and invented the hereditarians theory of intelligence.

Henry Herbert Goddard brought the Binet scale to America and popularized it as a measure of innate intelligence. He translated Binet's scales into English and agitated for their general use. But it was Lewis Terman of Stanford who really developed the Stanford Binet Scale as a measure of innate intelligence. Terman was interested in doing longitudinal studies of gifted children, which was the centerpiece of his career as a psychologist. He searched for ways in which he could assess individual differences so that he could determine the upper end of the distribution of ability or intelligence. With the introduction of the Binet by Goddard, Terman seized on this opportunity and produced the first widely used individual measure of intelligence in America—the Stanford Binet published in 1916. German psychologist William Stern expressed the total score earned on this scale as the intelligence quotient or IQ, a term he coined in 1912. IQ expresses the ratio of mental age (i.e., average test performance for a given age) to chronological age multiplied by 100. Although Terman did not create the concept of IQ, he is credited with introducing it in the United States.

Several controversial pieces of literature have appeared (in the literature) during the past several decades such as follows:

1. Arthur Jensen's *Harvard Educational* review article titled "How Much Can We Boost IQ and Scholastic Achievement?" (1969)

2. Jensen's *Bias in Mental Testing* (1980)
3. Charles Murray and Richard Herrnstein's *The Bell Curve* (1994)
4. J. Phillipe Rushton's *Race, Evolution, and Behavior* (1995)
5. Micheal Levin's *Why Race Matters: Race Differences and What They Mean* (1997)

Only two of these works (numbers 1 and 3) will be discussed in this paper.

Jensen's article created a firestorm of controversy about IQ testing of blacks and whites (Jensen 1969). His article provided twelve conclusions as follows:

1. IQ tests are valid and reliable measures of intelligence.
2. IQ is highly heritable—80 percent genetic and 20 percent environment.
3. Blacks score 15 points, on the average, lower than whites on IQ tests. The differences are genetically determined.
4. A mathematical model (statistical) exists to determine heritability (H2).
5. A dysgenic trend threatens our society; black genes are dysgenic.
6. Compensatory education has been tried and failed.
7. Two types of learning/intelligence exist:
    a. Level 1—abstract ability (whites excel in this ability).
    b. Level 2—associative learning or rote memory (blacks do better in this than level 1).
8. IQ tests are color-blind, that is, they show the same reliability and predictability for blacks as for whites.
9. There is no significant examiner effect on subject scores.
10. Occupational and scholastic success correlate well with IQ test scores.
11. Self-fulfilling prophecy (i.e., teacher expectations) is not a contributing factor for the lower IQ of blacks.
12. Malnutrition does not affect intelligence.

Jensen's article reignited the IQ controversy and made it a politically sensitive issue, particularly at the height of the civil rights movement. Criticisms came from everywhere. The most influential critique was provided by Leon Kamin in his 1974 book *The Science and Politics of IQ*. Kamin quotes extensively from the writings of the pioneers of IQ testing and shows how they held extreme hereditarian views, some of them quite viciously racist. Specifically, he showed how these pioneers argued in support of laws which were enacted in a number of states permitting eugenic sterilization of the feebleminded and also for the establishment of immigration quotas favoring the allegedly superior Nordic races.

The most spectacular feature of Kamin's analysis concerns the heritability studies of Sir Cyril Burt who was the dean of British psychometricians until his death in 1972. Burt's research played a key role in the arguments of Jensen and other hereditarians. Kamin showed that Burt's reports were seriously flawed and that his results contained a number of impossible correlations. Kamin stated further that "there exist no data which should lead a prudent man to accept the hypothesis that IQ test score are to any degree heritable" (Kamin 1974).

Although Kamin did not accuse Burt of fraud, a journalist Oliver Gillie, who provided evidence that the research assistants with whom Burt claimed to have conducted his research probably never existed, finally made the allegation of fraud in 1976 (Kamin 1974).

Another controversial piece of literature is *The Bell Curve* (Murray and Herrnstein 1994). Unlike the hostile reception to Jensen's work, Murray and Herrnstein's work seemed to have been more openly accepted within the ranks of the conservative elite.

Before I discuss *The Bell Curve* and its flaws, permit me to examine the two author's credentials. First, the late Richard Herrnstein was an experimental psychologist who received his doctorate in psychology from Harvard and taught there until his death. In 1971, he published a rather controversial article in *Atlantic Monthly*. In this article, he supported the notion of the heritability of IQ. His proposition, put in the form of a syllogism, was that because IQ is substantially heritable, and because economic success in life depends in part on economic success, it follows that social standing is bound to be based, to some extent, on inherited differences.

Further, Herrnstein's research was supported by the Pioneer Fund, an Aryan, i.e., racist organization. Until recently, the Pioneer's charter stated that it would award scholarships only to students deemed to be descended from white persons who settled in the original thirteen states. Professor Garland Allen of Washington University wrote a scholarly article on the history of the Pioneer and its racist activities.

Dr. Charles Murray is a graduate of MIT where he received his doctorate in political science. Psychology and political science are strange bedfellows. At the time of writing of *The Bell Curve*, Murray was a Bradley fellow at the American Enterprise Institute. His work was underwritten by a grant from the Bradley foundation that has been described as the nation's biggest underwriter of conservative intellectual activity. The Bradley Foundation supports one kind of work that with right wing, politically conservative value. To my knowledge, Murray has conducted no primary studies on intelligence. His works are built on the works of others. As one can see, these two scholars carry a great deal of political baggage, especially since conservative foundations supported their research. But their work and the works of others have public policy implications.

Dr. Asa Hilliard states that Herrnstein and Murray make a number of assumptions in their book that must be questioned (Hilliard 1995). These assumptions are:

1. that IQ tests created for mental measurement are universally applicable in a culturally plural and highly political world;
2. that IQ tests can measure mental capacity accurately;
3. that correlation is causation;
4. that human potential is correlated with certain behaviors such as crime, school achievement, welfare dependency, teenage pregnancy, and that these are explained by IQ;
5. that "intelligence" which is supposedly measured by IQ tests is stable and does not change; and

6. that there is equal opportunity to learn and common exposure to cultural experience for all.

Dr. Hilliard states that there are "eight cracks" in *The Bell Curve* as follows:

1. The first crack is that *The Bell Curve* is bad psychology. It does not reflect the state of the art in mental measurement.
2. The second crack in *The Bell Curve* is bad biology/anthropology. The authors use race and ethnicity interchangeably. Since ethnicity is a cultural concept, the genetic heritability of ethnicity makes no sense at all.
3. The third crack is bad pedagogy. There is an extensive body of literature that documents the power of schools to change students' achievement in significant ways. *The Bell Curve* does not reflect the state of art in the literature on effective schools.

Studies have demonstrated that although the average IQ of blacks and whites during their senior years in high school that whites tend to outscore blacks by as many as 15 IQ points. But send those students to college and the IQ of black students who graduate increases more than four times as much as those of the white college classmates, effectively cutting the black-white IQ gap in half. This is one of the key findings of two Washington University professors. They report the following: Our study shows that the differences in IQ test scores among blacks and whites may have little to do with genetics and much to do with relative quality of the educational opportunities afforded blacks and whites. The study began as a response to *The Bell Curve* which contends that blacks are genetically less intelligent than whites and that this intelligence gap cannot be greatly changed by education. Herrnstein and Murray argue that affirmative action programs in higher education offer diminishing returns because blacks lack the cognitive ability to benefit from advanced education at least to the same degree as whites and Asians. Our findings suggest that *The Bell Curve* substantially overstates the case for race-based intellectual differences because it ignored the important influence of the quality of elementary and secondary school on IQ test scores.

4. The fourth crack is the fact that schools do not all offer the same quality of education and that this inequity may significantly influence differences in IQ.
5. The next flaw in *The Bell Curve* misses taking into consideration the tremendous effect of culture and language in mental measurements. Many African American children do not speak mainstream English during their early years of school. They speak a "home language" that is vastly different from mainstream English.

That language is the language they have heard and learned from their grandmas, grandpas, mamas, and daddies. By the time they enter school, these children have internalized the basic features of the "home language." They do not know that they are not supposed to talk like that. They may even be penalized for speaking Ebonics.

Several studies have suggested how the use of Ebonics increased the test and reading scores of African American children. The first study translated (code switched) test items contained in a standardized test of basic concepts from standard English to Ebonics or into a language that was familiar to the children. The results were striking. The children who scored low on the standard English version performed exceptionally well on the Ebonics version (Williams 1997).

Here are two examples of how we changed the test items:

1. Standard English: Mark the toy that is behind the sofa.
    Ebonics: Mark the toy that is in back of the sofa.
2. Standard English: Point to the squirrel that is beginning to climb the tree.
    Ebonics: Point to the squirrel that is fixing to climb the tree.

In another study involving the Peabody Picture Vocabulary Test, Dr. Wendell Rivers translated the items from the standard version to an Ebonics version. Instead of asking the child to identify a *crib* as the test item required, the child was asked to identify a "baby bed." The term *crib* to many African American children meant an apartment. With the code switching, the children's IQ increased significantly (Williams and Rivers 1972).

What we discovered was that the standard versions contained *blocking agents* or noise. In many ways, the standard English version did not activate the black child's linguistic conceptual system. Rather the blocking agents or noise interfered with answering the question. This does not mean that the black child lacks the capacity to process standard language. Instead, the child's intake gates are not activated by the stimulus properties of standard English. The child must be taught to code switch—to move from Ebonics to standard English, just as an Asian or a Hispanic must be taught to move from the their native tongue to standard English. Dr. Savannah Young has provided an excellent book for teaching standard English to Ebonics speaking children. She provides exercises for parents and teachers to demonstrate how to help children learn standard English.

The last study using Ebonics was done by Dr. Gary and Charlesetta Simpkins. They developed a *Bridge program*. Bridge placed primary emphasis on initially using language skills already in the child's repertoire. Bridge is a process by which students proceed from the familiar (Ebonics) to the less familiar (standard English). It embraces the axiom, "Start where the child is." Bridge uses three readers to present the same story. One is written 100 percent in Ebonics, the second 50 percent Ebonics and 50 percent in standard English, and the third 100 percent in standard English. Two groups (a Bridge-exposed group and a non-Bridge group) were given two reading programs over a four-month period. At the end of the training period, they were given the Iowa Test of Basic Skills. The Bridge group showed a 6.2 months increase in their reading scores whereas the non-Bridge group reading scores increased only 1.6 months.

Teachers who were very cautious initially were enthusiastic after using the Bridge program.

Clearly, these studies demonstrate the effectiveness of recognizing and using the home language (in this case Ebonics) as a bridge to teach standard English.

6.   The sixth crack displays racism in research. Hilliard refers to the voluminous amount of literature of racism in the history of psychology and points out how *The Bell Curve* neglects to take this into consideration.

7.   The seventh crack reflects bad measurement. Hilliard stated that IQ testing is biased measurement and therefore *The Bell Curve* reflects bad science.

8.   The eighth crack is bad genetics. Hilliard states that *The Bell Curve* does not take into consideration the state of the art in the literature on genetics today, but it relies on reports of J. Phillipe Rushton, a psychologist from the University of Western Ontario. Rushton's work is politically conservative and very controversial (Hilliard 1995).

IQ tests have not fared well in the courts

In recent years, court action and legislation have been directed against tests in schools and industry. These actions have highlighted some of the uses and misuses of psychological tests. I will summarize some of the more important court cases and their consequences. They literally have taken a beating, yet they survive in this racist society.

One of the first court decisions in which tests figured prominently was Hobson v. Hanson in Washington, DC, which resulted in abolishing the track system. DC had three tracks for ability grouping, which resulted in a high degree of racial segregation within schools. Judge Skelly Wright gave the first legal decision against ability tests.

Another case was the Diana v. State Board of Education in California in 1970. This was a class action suit on behalf of all Mexican American children placed in EMR classes or who were scheduled to be given an IQ test. Diana, a little Mexican American girl, scored a

30 when administered by a white psychologist but scored 49 points higher when retested in Spanish. That case was settled out of court with the state of California agreeing:

1. to test all children in their primary language;
2. to assure that bilingual children currently enrolled in EMR classes be retested in their primary language on nonverbal tests;
3. that state psychologists develop an IQ test which reflects Mexican American culture; and
4. that Mexican American children be tested on the nonverbal or performance test items.

Because this was an out-of-court settlement, the state of California may have gotten off without honoring all of these agreements.

Black psychologists were very much aware of the increasing number of court cases that required a reexamination and extensive review of the value of IQ tests. In a fact sheet prepared by Dr. Harold Dent, a black psychologist described the Larry P. case. This is a premiere class action suit brought about by a group of black parents whose children were inappropriately classified as dumb and subsequently misplaced in classes for the educable mentally retarded. The suit contended that the civil rights of the black children guaranteed by the Fourteenth Amendment had been violated and that they had been denied equal opportunity to education guaranteed by the Civil Rights Act of 1964 and the California Educational Code.

On June 21, 1972, Judge Robert Peckham issued a preliminary injunction against the San Francisco Unified School District to enjoin the district from requiring the use of IQ tests that do not take into account the cultural and experiential background of black children. San Francisco School District appealed the decision, but in August 1973, the Ninth Circuit Court of Appeals upheld Judge Peckham's decision.

The parents went back to court and asked Judge Peckham to extend his injunction to the entire state of California on behalf of all black children who were inappropriately misplaced in EMR classes. On December 14, 1974, Judge Peckham extended the injunction to include all black children in the state of California who were inappropriately misclassified as EMR.

The Larry P. trial began on October 11, 1977, and final arguments were heard on May 30, 1978. The black psychologists involved were: Dr. Asa Hilliard, formerly dean of the College of Education at San Francisco State University; Dr. Gerald West, a Bay Area psychologist; Dr. William Pierce, a Bay Area psychologist; and Dr. Harold Dent, a Bay Area psychologist.

Almost a year and a half after the closing arguments (October 16, 1979), Judge Peckham issued his landmark decision:

1. that federal and state constitutional and statutory law had been violated;
2. that IQ tests were culturally biased and had not been validated for the purpose for which they were being used, i.e., the placement of black children in EMR classes; and
3. that the plaintiff's constitutional rights to equal education had been violated by wrongfully confining them to "dead-end" EMR classes.

The court therefore ordered the following injunctive relief:

1. The defendants are enjoined from utilizing or permitting the use of standardized intelligence tests for the identification of black EMR children or their placement into EMR classes without securing the approval of the court.
2. The defendants are hereby ordered to monitor and eliminate disproportional placement of black children in EMR classes. This remedy has relevance as the Oakland Unified School District black students comprise the majority of the Special Education classes.
3. To remedy the harm to black children who have been misidentified as EMR pupils and to prevent these discriminatory practices from recurring, the defendants shall

direct each school district to reevaluate every black child currently identified as an EMR child without including in the psychological evaluation a standardized intelligence or ability test.

A similar case in Chicago was Parents Against Special Education (PASE). The PASE case was also a class action one but did not receive the national press that Larry P. received. Initiated in 1974, it involved black and Hispanic students in EMR classrooms. The premise was the same as Larry P., to eliminate IQ tests as the sole determinant tor the placement of black and Hispanic students in EMR.

After long court sessions, Judge William Grady ruled that IQ tests were not in and of themselves discriminatory and that sufficient safeguards existed in the federal laws to reduce bias in decision making. Ironically, after that decision, the Chicago School Board passed a resolution to voluntarily discontinue the use of standardized tests in the screening and evaluation of special education students and agreed as part of a consent decree to reassess all EMR students in two years using a measure possessing local and independent norms.

Another area involving court cases is that used in professional selection and promotion. In Mississippi, they were using tests to hire and fire teachers. In that particular case, Armistead v. Starkville, the court ruled against using the Graduate Record Examination as a basis for hiring or firing teachers. The tests have lost in all of their battles.

Because of the Larry P. decision and other court decisions against tests, throughout the educational community people have been calling tor test publishers to be more accountable by supporting truth in testing legislation. In September 1978, former Governor Jerry Brown signed into law the nation's first truth in testing law (SB 2050). This legislation requires the following:

1. Test publishers to make available reports regarding the administration and use of standardized tests.
2. Test publishers to file copies of test questions and answers with California Postsecondary Education Commission as

well as information describing the psychometric quality of the test.
3.   Test publishers to send more information about a test to prospective test-takers.

On July 14, 1979, former Governor Hugh Carey of New York signed into law a truth in testing law. The intent of the bill is to make test subjects and persons who use test results more fully aware of the characteristics, uses, limitations, and potential misuses of tests and to allow students, educators, and public officials to scrutinize the production and administration of standardized tests. The bill further requires:

1.   test publishers to file copies of all background reports and statistical data pertaining to their tests with the Commissioner of Education; and
2.   that a copy of test questions and corresponding answers is filed with the Commissioner and that prospective test-takers be provided with a notice that provides substantial information about the test they are required to take.

As we approach the twenty-first century, this nation cannot afford to leave undeveloped the talents of millions of children who happen to be born different by virtue of race, language, sex, income status, or mental ability. Nor can this nation ignore, under the pretense of educational excellence, the unfinished national task of offering every child—black, Hispanic, native American, and white—an equal chance to learn and to become a self-sufficient and productive citizen.

It is my firm belief that education is a fundamental right deserving protection under the Fourteenth Amendment, which guaranteed all Americans equal protection of the law. Democracy does not guarantee success, but it is supposed to guarantee equal opportunity.

I further believe that progress for African Americans will accelerate when we are able to build on the knowledge provided by our ancestors and pass it on to the succeeding generations. When we forget this knowledge or when we do omit this information in our educational process or when this knowledge is distorted, whether by accident or design, a terrible condition is created. The late Dr. Bobby Wright called this condition mentacide or the deliberate destruction of a group's mind caused by the omission, distortion of the history, or otherwise misrepresenting the group's history with negative, deviant information.

One of my former students, Dr. Daudi Azibo, says that when we are miseducated a condition of misorientation is induced that one is confused about his or her identity. Thus, as we survey the historical and current state of affairs of African Americans, we notice a familiar litany of rather negative and pathological descriptions of African Americans. Words and phrases such as slavery, underprivileged, gangs, drugs, crime, unemployment, teenage pregnancy, school failure, school dropout, welfare, and a seemingly endless litany of descriptions of deficits and weaknesses. Although such tragic conditions do exist, they do not exist at the level as the media portrays it. For example, when I was in high school, ancient history was described as beginning in Greece. I did not know that ancient history began in Africa in Ghana, Songhai, and Mali. I was not told that the Greeks went down into Egypt with fogged minds and were taught advanced theology, philosophy, and cosmology. I was not taught about Imhotep who lived two thousand years before the Greeks came down. They did not teach me that Imhotep was perhaps the first multi-genius, a poet, philosopher, astronomer, engineer, and the world's first physician. When a group's history is omitted/distorted, we get a great deal of misinformation.

Carter G. Woodson said, "Lead people to believe certain fallacies, and you can control their minds and control their behind." They will do what they have been told to do. You create a lot of myths about these people that their families are broken down, that they are intellectually inferior, that they have self-hatred, and that they have bad language, and people will begin to internalize all this. The history is crushed.

The sum total of all of this is that the children are miseducated, disoriented, and confused. A non-racist education would teach children that Egypt is in Africa, not in the Middle East. When you have a background of racism in the country, there are efforts to justify this.

People have come out to prove that we are inferior. In a little study that was done in Texas, a brilliant son of an African American father was placed in special education. The father raised Cain and said, "What's happening here?"

They found that 75 percent of the black students failed and 66 percent of the Hispanic students, but only 37 percent of the white students failed because the black students and Hispanic students were going into special education. When they were retested by black, none of these students were placed in special education. There must be some kind of conspiracy out here to put black students in special education. There are efforts now to discredit what we do.

I was reading about the two black women doctors who delivered the first sextuplets. They are proud to say they are products of affirmative action. But there are people like Ward Connerly who want to end affirmative action. But these products of affirmative action delivered the first sextuplets.

Amid the crises, problems, and challenges, we have many, many success stories and the unbridled ability to meet those challenges, overcome those problems, and transform the crises into open doors of opportunity for our collective advancement. I believe when we write our history, Afrocentrically, we will have a different group of African American citizens. Afrocentric education is a systematic and comprehensive method of equipping our people with the will and skills necessary to effectively solve the problems and meet the challenges that confront our people and humankind.

If our black men and women, our black boys and girls can be super athletes and gold medalists, they can become super businessmen and women, doctors, lawyers, accountants, and all the high-level positions. It is time to develop black scholars and black scholar-athletes. I want to see scholastic trophies rather than athletic trophies in the halls of elementary and high schools.

Let me close with a metaphor that will illustrate the point of how testing is continued in this country. I call the metaphor, "The Apes Way of Perceiving the World."

Start with a cage containing five (5) apes. In the cage, hang a banana on a string and put stairs under it. Before long, an ape will go to the stairs and start to climb toward the banana. As soon as he touches the stairs, spray all of the apes with ice cold water. After a while, another ape makes an attempt with the same result; all of the apes are again sprayed with ice cold water. Soon, all of the apes realize that if any one of them approaches the stairs, they all will be sprayed with ice cold water. Now, turn off the ice cold water. If later, another ape tries to climb the stairs, the other apes will try to stop him, even though no water is sprayed on them. Now remove one ape from the cage and replace it with a new one. The new ape sees the banana and tries to climb the stairs. To his horror, all the other apes attack him. After another attempt and attack, he knows that if he tries to climb the stairs, he will be assaulted. He does not try to climb the stairs again.

Next, remove another of the original five apes and replace it with a new one. The newcomer goes to the stairs and is beaten senseless. Surprisingly, the previous newcomer takes part in the punishment with enthusiasm.

Again, remove another of the original apes and replace it with a new one. The new ape makes it to the stairs and is attacked as well. Two of the four apes that beat the new ape have no idea why they were not permitted to climb the stairs or why they are participating in the beating of the newest ape.

Now remove the fourth and fifth of the original apes. All original apes that were sprayed with cold water have been replaced. Nevertheless, no ape ever again approaches the stairs. Why not?

"Because that's the way it's always been done." Just because IQ tests have been the way our abilities are measured, are we going to continue in that manner into the next millennium?

CHAPTER
2

Legal Issues in Testing African Americans

John Affeldt

Thanks to all of you for this opportunity to talk about legal issues on the use of the IQ test for African Americans. Public Advocates began litigating the Larry P. case in the early '70s. I was not on the case at that point. I was in the first or second grade then. I'm now the lead counsel on the Larry P. case and the lead counsel on probably the current major testing litigation in the country which is Public Advocates's challenge to the California Basic Educational Skills Test (CBEST), which is California's teacher certification examination for anyone who wants to be a teacher, counselor, principal, or have any job in public education. Anyone who wants to teach in California public schools has to pass the CBEST. By the state's own admission, the CBEST is the primary reason we have an 80 percent white teaching force and a 60 percent nonwhite student population and also the primary reason we're short some twenty thousand bilingual teachers in our schools.

The Larry P. case started because members such as Drs. Harold Dent, Asa Hilliard, William Pierce, Gerald West, and Robert Williams began a frontal attack on the IQ test and the use of the IQ test for the identification and placement of individuals in special education, particularly African Americans in special education—its most frequent use.

People looked around and saw there was a huge overrepresentation of African Americans in special education programs which still continues to be the case. In California, we decided to challenge that practice of placing African Americans in educable mentally retarded classes or EMR classes based on the results of IQ tests, believing that these tests underrepresented the intelligence of African American children, leading to the their overrepresentation in EMR classes.

EMR classes were not classes for the severely mentally retarded but for those who were mildly mentally impaired. Essentially, these were not the most severe EMR children.

Now those children would be placed in learning disabled classes. As cases like Larry P. came along, legislation passed in Congress in the 1970s to revamp special education. Because it was socially less acceptable to label someone mentally retarded, students were shifted into the learning disabled category.

In the early 1970s, African Americans made up 25 percent of the students in EMR classes statewide though they were only 10 percent of the student population statewide. In the twenty districts that contained 80 percent of the African American student population, 62 percent of EMR classes consisted of African American students and only about 28 percent of the overall student population was African American. There were two and a half to three times the percentage of African Americans in EMR as in the student population.

EMR classes were a dead end, as the court found. EMR students were not given any hope of ever being mainstreamed. The purpose of EMR was not to teach academic content. The purpose was to teach "social adjustment" or "economic usefulness," "basic home and community living skills," "grooming skills," and personal hygiene. A placement in EMR was a lifelong sentence to underemployment.

With the Larry P. case, IQ tests were scrutinized more closely than they ever have been in any other forum. It remains the best adversarial scrutiny of IQ tests with a six-month trial, ten thousand pages of trial transcript and thousands of exhibits.

And at the end, the court concluded that IQ tests cannot truly define, much less measure intelligence and that the tests that the court examined were racially and culturally biased against African Americans and were not ever validated for placing African Americans in special education programs, particularly EMR programs. The court examined the notorious genetic argument and rejected it. No evidence was there to indicate that African Americans were inherently intellectually inferior to whites. Instead, the court recognized, as Dr. Robert Williams noted earlier, that the history of IQ testing is not a neutral scientific endeavor but has been one motivated by racial prejudice, social Darwinism, and use of scientific mystique to seek to legitimate such racial prejudice.

In examining how specifically IQ tests are discriminatory against African Americans, the court realized that the tests are normed on white middleclass children. This predominant cultural norm invaded the test so that the test is measured not against your innate intelligence but against your acquisition of knowledge, your acquisition of learned information over the course of your life.

And if your test is based on white middle-class children, then African American children from a non-middle-class background aren't going to perform as well. Dr. Asa Hilliard testified that black people have a cultural heritage that represents an experience pool that is never used or tested in IQ tests.

It is interesting to note that when girls performed differently than boys on IQ tests, they changed the test. They said something must be wrong because girls aren't inherently intellectually inferior to boys. But when African Americans or Latinos performed substantially poorer, they didn't change the test. Instead they concluded that the test was working.

The evidence also shows that IQ tests have very little practical use. They don't predict actual performance in the classroom, and more importantly, they predict less accurately for African Americans than they do for whites. In fact, grades for African Americans were a better predictor of how an African American was going to do in subsequent schooling than using the test. Even if the IQ test could predict some things, it was a much poorer predictor for African

Americans than it was for whites. That meant that more errors would be made for African American children than for white children, and the court found that unacceptable.

The Larry P. case was a landmark ruling in 1979 and was upheld by the Ninth Circuit Court of Appeals in 1986. Larry P. has been attacked by the right wing and some parts of the testing industry. The problem with this is that most of these attacks are not coming from African American folks or poor people. They are coming from the testing industry which invested heavily into repudiating Larry P. after the judgment.

There's a big National Academy of Sciences study that was done and you've got *The Bell Curve* coming out. There's a right wing legal foundation from Kansas City called the Landmark Legal Foundation that attacked Larry P. in 1988 in a lawsuit called Crawford v. Honig. They have asserted in that case that African American children have a right, a constitutional right to an IQ test, a constitutional right to be discriminated against by a biased IQ test. That's not how they framed it, but their argument was that African Americans were being denied access to IQ tests and white kids were not. The court never agreed with that or reached that argument.

The Landmark folks also argued that Larry P. only applied to EMR classes or their "substantial equivalent" and that there now were no EMR classes in California or their substantial equivalent. You see in the 1980s, the EMR program was phased out in California and different categories were introduced, the primary one being learning disabled where most African Americans now are. The court concluded that maybe we do need to determine what is the current substantial equivalent of the old EMR category in California. That issue still remains. There hasn't been any trial or hearing set but that is still on the court's docket to have a follow-up hearing on the current substantial equivalent of EMR in California.

In the meantime, the State Department of Education has issued an advisory to school districts to continue not to give IQ tests to place an African American students in special education. That's the current status quo of Larry P. While we got Larry P., the courts are not a reliable ally in this struggle. It is not advisable to place all one's eggs in one basket such that if we don't like the test, just sue and expect the courts to stop its use. Courts, as conservative institutions, are reluctant to attack tests and to strike them down and that's more true now than it was in the 1970s.

With the CBEST exam for example, the evidence showed that race was the single biggest factor of who was going to pass the test. It's a bigger factor than grade point averages or what kind of school or university you went to or what courses you majored in or whether or not English is your first language. Race was the single most important factor. The main argument against the CBEST wasn't that the test was biased but that it was meaningless. It didn't tell you anything about who's going to be an effective teacher or counselor or administrator. It certainly hadn't been examined in that light. So why are we continuing to use it? In fact, the CBEST is a pseudo-IQ test. It's trying to measure people's reasoning ability. There's one test for about twenty-five different job positions, and you can't really measure twenty-five different jobs at one time, so they're trying to abstractly measure someone's reasoning or cognitive skills. Even the state admits that it's not valid for that purpose. But I really think that is the underlying purpose and how it's being used.

The state itself finally did a study and admitted that 80 percent of the math test is not job related. This is after fifteen years of failing people on the math test. The court nonetheless said there were no problems with the CBEST test and that case is on appeal. We should have a decision from the Court of Appeals sometime this year. Keep in mind that fighting discriminatory tests in this country is at least as much a political battle as it is a legal one.

In terms of the IQ debate, there's no quick alternative test. That's what people generally ask. If you don't use IQ test, then what test should we be using? Asa Hilliard (1995) said it best, "Why fixate on IQ and the alternatives to IQ because ultimately IQ tests have failed African Americans? They have not been useful. They have not helped improve educational outcomes of African American children."

Special education has not helped improve educational outcomes for African Americans overall. African Americans are still overrepresented in special education, and special education is still a dead end.

Most black children do not get mainstreamed back into the main-stream curriculum. By the time they graduate, their SAT scores are still lower than their white counterparts, so we're back at the same cycle.

My response to the people in this whole IQ question is that we really need to shift the paradigm to stop thinking about how to test people to identify their disabilities. What kind of label are we going to put on this child? Are we going to call him learning disabled? Mentally retarded? Speech or language disordered?

What we should be doing is trying to assess. It doesn't necessarily mean through a paper and pencil test but that can be part of the process. What we should assess is how they learn, not what's wrong with them. How does this child construct meaning? How does that child decode language and how does he learn? Then you construct an educational strategy around teaching that child in a unique way. There is now a large data base of effective schools around the country that makes no use of mental measurement. You have to ask with that large data base out there, if we know how to do it right, why aren't we doing it?

IQ and the Courts: Larry P. v. Wilson Riles and PASE v. Hannon

Asa G. Hilliard (Georgia State University)

This paper presents a brief history and a comparative analysis of two recent major federal court cases on standardized IQ testing and black children. It includes a discussion of some major implications of the two court decisions and a pending appeal. Finally, shortcomings of the two court battles are cited and suggested future directions for IQ psychometry and education are suggested.

In 1971, the National Association for the Advancement of Colored People supported a class action suit against Wilson Riles, superintendent of Public Instruction for California, the California

State Department Board of Education, and the San Francisco School Board over the placement of the following black children into classes for the mentally retarded: Darryl Lester, Sylvia Marie Walker, James Lanigan, Michael Sears, and John Harvey. The Bay Area Association of Black Psychologists led by Drs. William Pierce and Harold Dent reexamined children who had been placed into classes for the educable mentally retarded (EMR) using the same tests as had been used before but varying procedures to establish rapport. They found none of the children to be retarded. The case came to trial in 1977 and was decided in favor of the plaintiffs in Judge Robert F. Peckham's Ninth District Federal Court in San Francisco in 1980. This case is known as Larry P. v. Wilson Riles.

A similar class action suit was initiated in Chicago by a group of parents. It was called Parents in Action on Special Education (PASE). The case is referred to as PASE v. Hannon, Hannon being the superintendent of schools in Chicago at the time.

In both cases, it was alleged that standardized IQ tests were primarily responsible for the placement of the children in EMR classes and that the standardized IQ tests were racially and culturally biased against black children, causing them to be placed inappropriately in EMR classes.

In San Francisco, Judge Robert Peckham ruled in favor of the plaintiffs against the use of IQ tests. In Chicago, Judge John F. Grady ruled in favor of the defendants and for the IQ tests as he modified them. The San Francisco decision is being appealed. The Chicago case is not being appealed.

The final decision may come at the Supreme Court level. It will be a landmark decision since it could result in the extension of the California ban on the use of IQ tests to place black children into EMR classes. Even without a final decision, professional practice in the use of IQ tests in education is being carefully reevaluated (Holtzman, Heller, and Messick 1980; Wigdor and Gamer 1982). Without IQ tests, new ways for determining EMR placements would have to be created, or the whole EMR classification might need to be reevaluated to determine its educational utility and benefit.

It is the purpose of this paper to provide an overview of the cases to present a comparison of them and to analyze the extent to which these cases address the complete range of essential issues associated with IQ testing and black children for educational purposes.

At issue for black children is the matter of appropriate and meaningful assessment. In the background hangs the old issue of the genetic capacity of black people (Jensen 1980). Also at issue is the validity of IQ psychometry for education, public credibility for psychologists, and perhaps even the validity of special education pedagogy.

The existing IQ testing system as used in education is a ranking and classification system. It is not a diagnostic and remedial system. If remediation of learning difficulties or low-academic achievement is possible (Feuerstein 1979–1980), a major shift in professional orientation and practice is required. If remediation of such things as educable mental retardation (EMR) is not possible, then the burden of proof for the benefits of such sorting remains with advocates of such a system. In the absence of demonstrable benefits, one must question the use of such a system.

The cases

When Judge Robert F. Peckham found for the plaintiffs in the case of Larry P. v. Wilson Riles in the United States Federal District Court in San Francisco, he found IQ tests to be biased against black children.

We must recognize at the outset that the history of the IQ test and of special education classes built on IQ testing is not the history of neutral scientific discoveries translated into education reform. It is, at least in the early years, the history of racial prejudice of social Darwinism and of the use of the scientific "mystique" to legitimate such prejudices (Peckham 1979, 8).

In another United States Federal District Court in Chicago in a similar case, Judge John F. Grady found for the defendants. He rendered a decision that IQ tests, though somewhat biased, would have no appreciable effect on placement decisions: "I conclude that the possibility of the few biased items on these tests causing an EMR placement that would not otherwise occur is practically nonexistent" (Grady 1980, 101).

A close examination of both written opinions will show that IQ psychometry actually lost in both cases. First, it lost when Judge Robert F. Peckham found the tests to be culturally and racially biased against black children. In doing so, he appeared to be persuaded by the testimony of the plaintiffs' expert witnesses.

In the PASE v. Hannon case, although Judge John F. Grady ruled for the defendants, he did so only after declaring a plague on both pro and con houses of the expert witnesses. Moreover, Judge Grady took the extraordinary step not only of rejecting expert opinion, but by doing so, demonstrating a basic lack of respect for the professional expertise in the field by taking the position that his lay opinion about IQ tests was actually superior to both sets of professional opinion. The Peckham decision was a model of judicial restraint. Although Judge Peckham was not persuaded that IQ tests were valid for black children, he did not move beyond that position and attempt to establish a professional remedy for the difficulties. Indeed in his decision, he made explicit his uneasiness about having to enter the domain that should be left to professionals.

A second essential caveat is that there should be no illusion about our capacity as a court to require educational systems to transcend societal inequalities and provide black children generally with the kind of skills necessary for educational and social advancement in our country. That would take a major commitment, not a court order. We are perfectly aware of the complexity and interrelationship of educational problems and indeed of the danger that an attack on EMR classes, in the absence of effective remedial education, could even hurt those individuals who, despite the aims and approach of EMR classes in general, actually benefited from what appears in retrospect to have been misplacement. Nevertheless, that consideration cannot allow us to sanction a labeling process that unjustifiably blames educational failure on the ostensible mental retardation of black children and dooms disproportionate numbers of black children to a program designed to keep their performance below normal (Peckham 1979, 102).

Judge Grady expressed no such hesitation. Not only did he feel himself competent to make an item-by-item assessment of the presence or absence of cultural bias in IQ testing, but in the act of doing so, he placed into the public record the actual items on one of the Wechsler intelligence tests, making them publicly available for the first time. The net result of both decisions is that IQ testing was not known to make a contribution to education that would be convincing to a lay judge. Judge Peckham rules that IQ tests were biased based on his view of the testimony that was presented. Judge Grady rejected basic IQ testimony and made himself, a lay judge, superior to professional practice by "fixing the tests"!

The essence of the decisions

In the case of Larry P. v. Wilson Riles, six important points emerged from Judge Robert F. Peckham's decision. They are as follows:

1. The judge assumed that the actual differences in intellect between blacks and whites should be expected to be zero. Judge Peckham found no compelling evidence to justify any other assumption although the California State Department of Education officials expressed a different view.

A number of key state officials in addition testified that they were familiar with Professor Jensen's writings and they would not rule out the genetic explanation for disparities between white children in IQ scores and EMR enrollment.

IQ tests can only be explained as the product of the impermissible and scientifically dubious assumption that black children as a group are inherently less capable of academic achievement than white children.

Key officials in the State Department of Education, more-over, actually corroborated this explanation. They testified that they believed the over-enrollment of black and Chicano children in EMR classes accurately reflected the incidence of mental retardation among those children (Peckham 1979, 42, 88).

In the Chicago case, apparently the witnesses were able to agree on a zero difference among groups: "Defendants agreed with the plaintiffs that there is no evidence to support a hypothesis that blacks have less innate capacity than whites" (Grady 1980, 92).

2. Judge Peckham ruled that IQ tests were both racially and culturally biased.
3. Judge Peckham actually expressed the opinion that the tests were not valid for black children, but no compelling evidence was cited to establish the validity (except predictive validity) of IQ tests for white or other children.
4. Serious questions were raised, in the judge's opinion, regarding the validity of special education pedagogy, the "treatment" that is supposed to be rendered to children who are identified by the tests as educable mentally retarded. No empirical evidence was presented of specific benefit for children because of placement of children into classes for the educable mentally retarded.

Whatever the future, however, it is essential that California's educators confront the problem of the widespread failure to provide an adequate education to underprivileged minorities such as the black children who brought this lawsuit. Educators have too often been able to rationalize inaction by blaming educational failure on an assumed intellectual inferiority of disproportionate numbers of black children. That assumption without validation is unacceptable and is made all the more invidious when "legitimated" by ostensibly neutral, scientific IQ scores. We have refused to allow the continuation of EMR policies consistent only with that assumption, and it is hoped that this will clear the way for more constructive educational reform (Peckham 1979, 109–110).

In the words of Fred Hanson, a special education consultant and one of the key state administrators, "Slow learning must be caused by limited intellectual capacity." These classes are not meant for remedial instruction... Further, the curriculum was not and is not designed to help students learn the skills necessary to return to the regular instructional program. To quote again from the state handbook,

> The primary/instructional goals for the mentally retarded are set forth in the Education Code, Section 6902 as "Social Adjustment" and "Economic Usefulness." These primary goals should include physical health and development, personal hygiene and grooming, language and communication skills, social and emotional adjustment, basic home and community living skills, and citizenship. Every classroom activity should contribute in some meaningful way to achieving these goals... The educational goals for the educable mentally retarded are not reading, writing, and arithmetic per se; if these skills are accepted as the primary goals, then EMR students should remain in regular classes where academic skills are emphasized. (Peckham 1979, 17)

5. The judge expressed the opinion that the California State Department of Education was guilty of systematic and continuing negligence in the face of constant challenges to the validity of IQ testing for cultural minority populations.

In addition, while the SDE (State Department of Education) has dutifully collected the reports legally required from school districts about local disproportionate enrollment and it has required local boards to comply with the law and explain the variances, these reports have been treated in a manner calculated to maximize tolerance of minority disproportion. First, the SDE interpreted statutory requirements of a report when there is a variance of "15 percent or more from the percentage of such children in the district as a whole" to mean that a district was "entitled" to 15 free percentage points added to the minority representation in the population. Parity, therefore, was not even sought, and the literal reading of the statute meant that a district with 2 percent black children in the population could have 17 percent black enrollment in EMR classes. A district with 85 percent black children would in turn be allowed 100 percent of the EMR enrollment. Beyond these remarkably tolerant interpretations…the SDE never evaluated the adequacy of the local explanation for the disproportion and never sought to utilize the data or explanations to obtain a sounder understanding of the problem, much less to work toward a solution (Peckham 1979, 90–91).

The facts permit but one inference, and the State has not offered evidence that permits any other inference. Despite the admitted problems with the IQ tests, and despite disproportionate enrollments which have even been condemned by the legislature, the SDE's actions reveal a complacent acceptance of those disproportions and that complacency was evidently built on easy but unsubstantiated assumptions about the incidence of retardation or at least low intelligence among black children. Coupled with the affirmative decision to adopt a requirement of particular IQ tests in 1969, that complacent acceptance must be seen as a desire to perpetuate the segregation of minorities in inferior, dead end, and stigmatizing classes for the retarded (Peckham 1979, 92).

6. The judge virtually begged professionals to do their homework in such a way that the case could be taken out of the court arena.

Judge Grady explicitly stated that he was unimpressed by expert witnesses on either side of the question:

> The testimony, standing alone, does not
> preponderate in either direction. I have seen cases
> in which one set of experts is clearly more credi-

> ble than the others and will, by their demeanor, appearance, credentials, and the reasonableness of their testimony, carry the day. This is not such a case. None of the witnesses in this case has so impressed me with his or her credibility or expertise that I would feel secure in basing a decision simply on his or her opinion. In some instances, I am satisfied that the opinions expressed are more the result of doctrinaire commitment to a preconceived idea than they are the result of scientific inquiry. I need something more than the conclusions of the witnesses in order to arrive at my own conclusions. (Grady 1980, 8)

He appeared to feel quite comfortable that he could find culturally biased items on his own by a simple process of inspection:

> It is obvious to me that I must examine the tests themselves in order to know what the witnesses are talking about. I do not see how an informed decision on the question of bias could be reached in any other way for me to say that the tests are either biased or unbiased without analyzing the test items in detail would reveal nothing about the tests but only something about my opinion of the tests… I have said enough to indicate my belief that an analysis of the tests is essential. I will now proceed to that task. (Grady 1980, 8–9)

Having "repaired" the damage which he perceived, Judge Grady was apparently of the opinion that his "revised Wechsler" was valid. Consequently at that point, we actually had a new IQ test in Chicago—the Grady-Wechsler!

The limitations of the two court cases

Neither the Larry P. v. Wilson Riles nor the PASE v. Hannon cases offered an opportunity for a true test of the validity of IQ tests:

> We do not address the broader questions of whether these IQ tests are generally valid as measures of intelligence, whether individual items are appropriate for that purpose or whether the tests could be improved. (Grady 1980, 91–92)

Even if they had, traditional professional criteria for validity determination are inadequate since whole categories of relevant data are never developed or brought to bear on the process of establishing test validity. Because of the way in which the initial Larry P. v. Wilson Riles complaint was developed, no real attention was paid to the weaknesses in the validity criteria. In the case of Larry P. v. Wilson Riles, black children were retested by black psychologists on the same IQ instrument after the black psychologists made certain adjustments to account for the cultural background of the children and to ensure the establishment of rapport between examiner and examinee. Since the results were different for the children on the second administration of the same test, it was alleged that the tests were culturally biased against black children. By choosing to select the dimension of the cultural bias as the basic basis for challenging the validity of the IQ tests in the Larry P. v. Wilson Riles and PASE v. Hannon cases, the plaintiffs in both cases virtually guaranteed a narrowly restricted domain within which the validity battle would be fought. I regard this as unfortunate since while it is my opinion that the cultural bias is not the root problem with standardized IQ tests, cultural bias is but the symptom of the more deeply rooted problem of test validity itself. Do standardized IQ tests actually measure mental functions or the ability to learn in any or all populations?

In order to gain some appreciation for the vastness of the relevant domain that is excluded from cultural bias and instructional validity determination at present, we may focus on categories of missing data. Some of them are as follows:

1. No data on treatment ("school"). The absence of a systematically developed operational definition of "school" or "instruction" in studies of the validity of IQ tests leaves a critical variable in the study of test validity uncontrolled. Such data as do exist of variations in the quality of instructional treatment among teachers and among schools indicate that wide variation exists. These variations in treatment (teaching quality) may be sufficient to explain virtually all of the differences between cultural groups that psychometrists find when measuring IQ differences, especially if we include data both on school and on certain other major environmental treatments such as television exposure and economic opportunity. The major point is that IQ test makers and advocates do not deal with these variables at all.
2. No data on language and the application of linguistic criteria in test development.

In the '50s, the United States government spent millions of dollars developing systems for machine translation of Russian and other languages. After years of effort on the part of some of the most talented linguists in the country, it was finally concluded that the only reliable, and ultimately the fastest, translator is a human being deeply conversant not only with the language but with the subject as well. The computers could spew out yards of printout but they meant very little. The words and some of the grammar were all there, but the sense was distorted. That the project failed was not due to lack of application, time, money, or talent, but for other reasons, which are central to the theme of this chapter.

The problem lies not in the linguistic code but in the context, which carries varying proportions of the meaning. Without context, the code is incomplete since it encompasses only part of the message. This should become clear if one remembers that the spoken language is an abstraction of an event that happened, might have happened, or is being planned. As any writer knows, an event is usually infinitely more complex and rich than the language used to describe it. Moreover, the writing system is an abstraction of the spoken system and is in effect a reminder system of what somebody said or could have said. In the process of abstracting, as contrasted with measuring, people take in some things and unconsciously ignore others. This is what intelligence is—paying attention to the right things (Hall 1977, 86–87).

The use of a common language, specifically common English, is the essential vehicle for interrogation, responding, and interpretation of standardized IQ test scores. Therefore, an understanding of the science of linguistics, particularly in this case as it applies to the language of African Americans, is vital to any "science" of intellectual measurement that is dependent upon language, especially as such language varies from the general language of Americans. It is a gross scientific error to ignore the application of cultural linguistic principles to the analysis of interrogation, responding, and interpretation in standardized IQ testing.

3. No data on culture. Like language, culture (which includes language) is a category of systematic scientific study. The existence of culture, the principles of its operation, and the existence of specific cultural configurations such as African American culture, including its variations, is well known to students of culture or to students of African American culture. Abundant empirical data exist that must be taken into account systematically when examining interrogation, responding, and interpretation of IQ data, which essentially are narrow cultural data. Test makers do not do this. There is no evidence that they can.

4. No data on the impact of IQ on instruction. The present limited justification for the use of IQ testing is made through an appeal to predictive validity. The gaping deficit in such an approach is that no empirical data exist to demonstrate that the systematic and correct use of IQ tests

(predictive validity or not) results in instructional benefits to children. This is a fundamental error since even if a weak predictive association exists between IQ and school achievement, the pedagogical value of doing IQ testing must be demonstrated by reference to data on improved academic outcomes for children as a consequence of the use of IQ tests.

5. No data on the impact of special education. During the trial, the benefits of special education were assumed by the defendants, not demonstrated. No empirical data were presented to show that the assignment of children to EMR (EMH in Chicago) classes on the basis of IQ tests or any other measure resulted in a better educational outcome for such children. Therefore, the absence of validity data on "EMR"/"EMH" instructions links with the absence of a pedagogically valid application for IQ tests.

6. No data on the impact of successful teaching. Given the fact that no operational definition of "school" treatment was given, it should not be surprising that no recognition was given to the fact that the quality of general teaching that is available to various children varies widely in quite systematic ways, ways that are associated with the cultural background of students. The actual validity of IQ tests can never be known in the face of psychometric ignorance regarding variations in the quality of teaching, EMR or "regular," to which various children are exposed who are to be compared on IQ test scores. We must have validity and reliability data on pedagogical treatments.

7. No data on early sensory-motor development of African and African American children. Any systematic review of the literature on the sensory-motor development of African and African American children will reveal a remarkable phenomenon, which must be explained, especially in view of the negative perception of the learning abilities of black children that is held by some writers. The repeated finding in the literature is that African and African American

children exceed the norms on tests of sensory-motor (both physical and cognitive) development during the first two years of life. At the time that the basic "culturally neutral" tests are changed, the early advantage of African and African American children appears to decline. Were we in possession of systematic data on language and culture, it is my opinion that this apparent decline could be explained quite easily. As early sensory-motor tests change to linguistically biased IQ tests, tests that are based on the language of middle America, we witness a change from relatively culture neutral to more culture-bound standardized assessment that creates a distortion in the comparisons of culturally different groups. To be valid, tests must be linguistically appropriate.

8. No experimental studies of differential "treatment" of educable mentally retarded. A rigorous validity test of standardized IQ measures could be conducted by taking a random sample of children who are identified by tests as educable mentally retarded and providing such children with systematic instructional treatment of a known high quality. A unique type of opportunity to examine "predictive validity" would then be presented. At present, predictive validity coefficients are earned by leaving everything in the school environment essentially free to vary (i.e., no reliability or validity data on "school"). Given the fact that the opportunities of different cultural groups in the United States can be documented to be systematically and distinctly different in quality, it is a scientific error to ignore the potential impact of such differential treatment on the instructional setting. Until the effects of differential treatments are ruled out by the use of experimental controls, no scientific answer to the cultural bias question can be given.

It should be clear from this list of neglected categories that testing the IQ tests for validity cannot be accomplished in ignorance of the data that must be generated within each of these categories. It should also be clear from the above why the charge of cultural bias in both IQ testing cases should have been the more basic charge that there was a lack of instructional validity for IQ tests. Clearly, the definitive court case on academic treatment in IQ testing has yet to be developed and did not exist in either the Larry P. v. Wilson Riles or the PASE v. Hannon case.

Why IQ testing cannot be fixed for school use

As indicated above, the problems with IQ testing are far more grave than cultural bias and the injuries resulting from their use extend beyond black children. The real questions is whether IQ testing contributes anything of significant value to the instructional and/or learning processes, such that we are better cuff with them than without. Up to now, responses to criticisms about IQ tests have generated the search for "culture-free," "culture-fair," "non-biased," "nondiscriminatory," and "alternative" tests of intelligence. Indeed, the language of Judge Peckham's remedy calls for such tests. One problem with such searches is that there seems to be an implicit assumption that whatever is wrong with IQ tests can be remedied by considering the tests in isolation from the instructional process that they are expected to serve. The problem is seen essentially as one restricted to and dealing solely with traditional psychometrics. This is unfortunate since it is the link or the question of the existence of a valid interaction between psychometrics and pedagogy that must be examined. This means that at least as much systematic attention must be paid to pedagogy as to psychometrics in any valid validation study.

The science of "mental measurement" may well be separated from the use of standardized IQ tests in school. It is possible that improvements in the science of mental measurement may occur without a direct practical application for pedagogy. It is also possible and has been demonstrated many times (Feuerstein 1980, Freire 1973, and Fuller 1977) that pedagogy can be drastically improved without reference to IQ testing at all. In other words, IQ testing in no way has been demonstrated to be either a prerequisite for successful instruction or even facilitative of instruction. If mental measurement is to mean anything at all for pedagogy, then psychometry is drastically in need of a paradigm shift. The need for such a paradigm shift should become obvious when we consider the problems with standardized IQ testing below:

1. The goal of IQ testing is wrong. The primary justification for the use of IQ testing in schools presently is to improve the "prediction of a child's future academic performance." As long as our present notion of predictive validity looms as large as the goal of psychometry in education, it is unlikely that the valuable tools of psychology for pedagogy can ever be brought to play in the educational situation. The acceptance of a predictive validity model in psychometry is also the acceptance of a notion of static intellectual stratification among the general population that is to be matched by static pedagogical stratification with the psychometrist performing in the role of fortune-teller.

2. The assumptions of IQ psychometry are wrong. As mentioned above, the assumptions are that members of the population can and need to be ranked by intellect and that such ranks are relatively stable. This is an article of faith, not science.

3. Present IQ psychometry suffers from the absence of an articulated concept of and operational definition of "teaching" or "school." Without such a concept and definition, adequate validity studies cannot be designed.

4. Present IQ psychometry suffers from the absence of a validated body of teaching practice. Valid systematic pedagogy is a prerequisite to the determination of valid pedagogical psychometry. For example, it does little good to prescribe "special education" to "educable mentally retarded children" when "special education" may be equally as varied in validity as well as strategies as "regular education."

5. Present IQ psychometry suffers from the fact that it has no valid link to instruction and never has had one.

6. Present IQ psychometry suffers from inadequate ancient criteria for determining test validity. At present, a test is considered "valid" if there is agreement with similar tests or if there is internal agreement within the test itself or if the test appears to be related to future academic performance. However, if the assumption underlying psychometry and pedagogy is changed from one of static learner and static learning conditions to changing learner and changing learning conditions, then radical changes are required in the concept both of validity and reliability. If effective teaching is expected to change the academic achievement of learners, then the expectation associated with present instrumentation must change. The new expectation is that predictive validity would be destroyed in many cases. Effective teaching can and does mean that the traditionally predicted outcomes for learners may not match actual attainment. Similarly, under conditions of effective pedagogy, the "reliability" of present instrumentation would also be destroyed. The concept of reliability is associated with stability in scores, and yet effective pedagogy is directed toward producing an instability, or more precisely, a change in achievement scores—even taking into account the comparisons among rates of change among learners. Clearly, for present IQ instrumentation, existing definitions of validity and reliability are totally inadequate if the educability rather than the ineducability of general population is assumed.

7. The problem definition with present IQ testing is wrong. As indicated above, it is neither "non-biased," "nondiscriminatory," "culture-fair," "culture-free," nor "alternative" testing which we seek. We seek valid testing, valid in the sense that a positive contribution is made to instructional outcomes. Each of these present problem definitions represents defensive tinkering with the IQ system without a basic willingness to engage in evaluation and change in the system itself.

What is needed in mental measurement

1. We need to change the goal. The goal in mental measurement must be to change the course of expected educational outcomes for children beyond what would be expected without psychometric intervention. Such a change in the goal for psychometry is associated with the need for companion goals in psychological and education treatment.
2. We need valid links between psychometry and pedagogy.
3. We desperately need a reconstruction of the concept and the criteria for test validity.
4. We need a reconstruction of the concept and criteria for test reliability.
5. To accomplish such drastic changes as implied in the above will require a redefinition of competency for psychometricians.
6. We need a drastic change in the role of psychometrists.

A review of the literature on mental measurement through the use of standardized IQ tests reveals what appears to be a studied unwillingness to confront certain types of issues. Unfortunately, these are the very issues that are critical when considering challenges to the validity of IQ tests as they are used in schools. Among these apparently forbidden issues are the following: What is the relationship of language to intellect? For example, what is "vocabulary"? What is it about vocabulary that makes it a measure of intellect? Is there a universal intellectual vocabulary? Similarly, we may examine cultural assumptions which ought to be made explicit. For example, what is "general information"? Is there a universal general information? What I am pointing to here is the absence of an articulated rationale for the inclusion of certain categories within IQ tests as well as the absence of a rationale for utilizing restricted versions of a particular language as the sole vehicle for interrogation, responding, and interpretation. Furthermore, it appears to be an invasion of taboo territory to ask psychometrists for an articulated description of the criteria that they use for item construction. There is a general willingness to look at the way different subjects respond on items that have been constructed but not to look at the rationale for item construction in the first place. Finally, beyond the factor analytically derived notion of present mental testing through IQ instruments gives information that causes discussants to be vague and amorphous in describing the mental functions that can or cannot be performed by test-takers.

Basically, IQ psychometry has given attention to areas in which it feels comfortable but studiously avoids the tough areas. At one time, it could have been said that there were minimal data to be consulted in such areas. However, that is far from true at this time. One can only read the apparent resistance to use such data or ignorance of the existence of such data as a fundamental deficiency in contemporary psychometry. It is most unfortunate that these were not the matters that were on trial in either the Larry P. v. Wilson Riles or PASE v. Hannon cases.

At this time, Wilson Riles and Henry P. Gunderson have filed an appeal to the opinion of Judge Peckham. Essentially, the appellants' position is but a rehash in slightly more detail of data that were presented at the trial. Appellants contest, without data, the ruling that IQ tests are culturally biased. In doing so, appellants appear to insist upon the very narrowly restricted meaning of the test bias that has been alluded to earlier:

> Appellant took the position that in judging
> bias in a test, one must use the legitimate; recog-
> nized definition of test bias; embraced by those
> who design and use tests namely its predictive
> validity that when the test of predictive validity is
> applied, the IQ tests are not biased and that they
> will predict equally well for blacks and whites the
> likelihood of success or failure in mastering the
> public school curriculum; that the EMR program
> is a benefit to pupils who are failing in school
> and require more individualized attention; that it
> need not be a permanent placement for the pupil
> who makes progress under that regimen; that

periodic reevaluations minimize the risk of mis-
classification; and that children are only placed
in the program when they meet all the eligibil-
ity criteria, including parental consent (Peckham
1981, 12).

If one takes the elements of the paradigm for criticism, which I
have suggested earlier, it is clear that appellants have done little more
than to give the routine response to any criticism of IQ tests. As I
have indicated, their whole argument rides on predictive validity.

As one reads the appellants' brief, especially where plaintiffs'
witnesses are quoted selectively, it is not clear from the interpretation presented that defendants understood the testimony of plaintiffs' witnesses. Certainly, the inferences that are drawn do not, in my
opinion, represent the essence of plaintiffs' testimony. Moreover, the
citations represent no systematic argument but rather what appears
to be random potshots at straw people who are created by the defendants' twisted interpretation of plaintiffs comments. One example
may suffice:

> Respondents, on the other hand, contend
> that the IQ test is not relevant because the class-
> room is not the only arena in which to display
> intelligent behavior. The ghetto drug pusher's
> business acumen is intelligent behavior. Knowing
> who Charlie Parker is intelligent behavior
> (RT208). Respondents want public school ori-
> ented definition of EMR to take into account
> many facets of human behavior which may be
> valuable, which have no relevance for the public
> schools. (Peckham 1981, 13)

I assume that intelligent functioning is independent of the particular content. I assume further than an IQ test is designed to be
a measure of intelligent functioning. At the same time, I recognize
that public school systems operate with particular academic content,

which will be quite distinct in some cases, from experiential content, which one may find in a variety of other public settings. No argument need be made that the content of any particular outside setting must be a part of the school experience, e.g., that the "ghetto drug pusher's business acumen" should be taught in the public schools. Surprisingly, the State seems unable to distinguish arguments about mental competence from arguments about curricular content. I certainly would not argue for the social desirability of drug pushing nor for the academic relevance to the school curriculum of the drug pusher's experience. But the legal, social, moral, or curriculum content problems associated with the drug pusher are quite distinct from the matter of intellectual functioning. If IQ testing is supposed to be simultaneously a measure of intellectual functioning and a measure of social desirability, moral values, legal action, etc., then such intent should be specified in the technical literature. Perhaps the inability of school people to distinguish intellectual from socially desirable behavior is one of the contributing factors to the low level of performance for many students in the public schools since they may be being treated for the wrong "malady."

The appellants' brief is poorly organized with citations of partial testimony of a variety of the State's witnesses on a variety of topics. Nothing new appears in this material. The State, led by such experts as Grossman and Humphreys, in its appeal has maintained its position that IQ tests are valid, leaving us with the inescapable conclusion that there is, as IQ tests describe, not only a 15-point difference in the average of IQ scores between black and white populations but that there is a comparable difference in inherent mentality as well.

Apparently stung by Judge Peckham's criticism that the State Department of Education was negligent in this matter, the opinion of the defendants offers weak citations regarding steps that it says were taken to respond to the charges of cultural bias. In doing so, it leans heavily on the master plan for special education that was developed by the State of California. Unfortunately, the master plan speaks to the issue of "mainstreaming" but does not speak to the issue of the disproportionate representation of blacks in classes for the educable mentally retarded. Furthermore, the State actually makes the claim in its brief that EMR placement is beneficial for the children who are so placed. It does so without any presentation of data that have been arrived at systematically. Neither are there systematic data to support the State's contention that significant numbers of students are returned to the mainstream as a result of excellent special educating and EMR classes.

There are several other things in the State's brief. However, in general, it is little more than a mishmash of citations that do not address the basic issues in the case, issues that have been described previously in this paper. In making the appeal, Wilson Riles et al. appear to be quite satisfied with the status quo, having argued in essence that it was simply meant to be. We see no forecasts on the part of the State to show that it expects that it or anyone else has the capability to ensure essential equity in the academic achievement of black and white students. After all the words have been cleared away, the meaning of the position taken by state superintendent of Public Instruction Wilson Riles and his codefendants is that they believe that black children are intellectually deficient and not simply educationally behind.

Conclusion

The fundamental issues in IQ psychometry have yet to be addressed. The Larry P. v. Wilson Riles and PASE v. Hannon cases simply serve as symptoms of the grave difficulties that exist in applied mental measurement in education. It took court cases to bring minimal problems with the IQ system to the surface, problems such as "cultural bias." What will it take to cause the profession itself to anticipate and avoid future difficulties by developing a focus now on the root problems associated with mental measurement applied to pedagogy? Just as defenders of IQ psychometry should find little to be happy about with the decision of Judge Grady, which apparently went in favor of the defendants, so should the whole field of psychology fail to find comfort in restricting its attention to the superficial issues that were addressed in the court cases.

Judge Peckham saw the problem but also wisely saw that a judge could speak merely to the legal aspects of such a problem, insisting upon constitutional guarantees of equal protection of the laws. Unlike Judge Grady, Judge Peckham knew that the actual reconstruction of professional practice ultimately can come only from enlightened professionals. That can happen only when the basic issues are on the table. Up to now, this has not been the case.

The split decision in these two court cases exposes a part of the problem. IQ psychometry has suffered a knockout since it was unable to demonstrate significant benefit for students. The basic problem with IQ psychometry is that the whole field rests on fundamentally erroneous assumptions about the abilities of learners and the nature of teaching. Clients have a right to expect a great deal from anyone who poses as a scientist or professional in psychology or education. As knowing professionals, our validity criteria for testing and teaching should be even more stringent than those found among the general public. Anointing or legitimating the obvious in education is hardly professional level work. Psychometrics must make a positive contribution to pedagogy.

Unfortunately, the standardized IQ tests are still on trial. One can hardly imagine a federal court trial to determine whether a missile launch from Cape Canaveral would be able to reach the moon. Even if such a trial was conducted, one would certainly not imagine a lay judge feeling competent enough to reject the opinion of space specialists and to construct his or her own spacecraft. I believe that this could be due to the fact that a fundamental respect for the achievements of space scientists has been built upon a demonstration of their competent performance. The chapter of competent performance has yet to be written in the story of psychometry and pedagogy.

CHAPTER 3

What Good Is This Thing Called Intelligence and Why Bother to Measure It?

Asa G. Hilliard (Georgia State University)

This article contains a review of issues and documentation concerning the possibility of "measuring" the intelligence of students. The construct validity of "intelligence," the role of cultural context as a modifier of the meaning of test results, and the lack of meaningful predictive validity of IQ tests are discussed. A discussion of the utility of the intelligence construct and IQ measures and their relationship to the design of beneficial pedagogy follows. Based on reviews of empirical evidence, it is concluded that the measurement of intelligence as practical, at present, makes no contribution to the design of instruction that is beneficial to students, as far as academic achievement is concerned. The main effects of the present popular intelligence measures are found to be negative.

Our ultimate message is a strikingly simple one. The purpose of the entire process—from referral for assessment to eventual placement in special education—is to improve instruction for children. The focus on educational benefits for children became our unifying theme, cutting across disciplinary boundaries and sharply divergent points of view.

These two things—the validity of assessment and the quality of instruction—are the subject of this report. Valid assessment, in our view, is marked by its relevance to and usefulness for instruction (Holtzman 1982, x–xi).

While academic failures are often attributed to characteristics of learners, current achievement also reflects the opportunities available to learn in school. If such opportunities have been lacking or if the quality of instruction offered varies across subgroups of the school-age population, then school failure and subsequent EMR referral and placement may represent a lack of expose to quality instruction for disadvantaged or minority children (Heller, Holtzman, and Messick 1982, 18).

The IQ test's claim to validity rests heavily on its predictive power. We find that prediction alone, however, is insufficient evidence of the test's educational utility. What is needed is evidence that children with scores in the EMR range learn more effectively in a special program or placement as argued in more detail in Chapter 4. We doubt that such evidence exists although we are not prepared as a panel to advocate the discontinuation of IQ tests. We feel that the burden of justification lies with its proponents to show that in particular cases, the tests have been used in a manner that contributes to the effectiveness of instruction for the children in question (Heller et al. 1982, 61).

Author's note: This article is based on a presentation made/or the National Council on Measurement in Education and the American Education Research Association symposium on the measurement of intelligence, April 1994. Direct all correspondence regarding this article to Asa G. Hilliard. Educational Policy Studies, Georgia State University, 33 Gilmer St SE, Atlanta, GA 30303-9983. *Journal of Black Psychology* volume 20 number 4, November 1994 430–444 © 1994 The Association of Black Psychologists.

I must state at the outset that I come to the discussion of the utility of "intelligence" testing and the utility of the intelligence construct from the point of view of an educational psychologist interested in the improvement of education. I recognize that there can be many reasons for interest in the human mind and how it functions and that some psychologists and others will be interested in "measuring" whatever is possible to be measured, perhaps just for its own sake.

Of course, the question of the utility of mental measurement can easily be divorced from the question of whether intelligence can be measured simply for the sake of doing it. It is also clear that, in a free society, scientists ought to be able to pursue any interesting question for which they can find support, or which they can do on their own, so long as they do no harm. So research to determine if such a thing as intelligence exists and, if it does, what its nature is, is likely to continue, and I have no quarrel with that.

However, major concerns arise when psychometricians and others move beyond inquiries about human intellect to the application of their science to the area of human problem solving. It is at this point that we must be concerned about the validity of connections between mental measurement and success in problem solving in teaching and learning.

For many reasons, some of them obvious, the primary focus of my critique is on the use of mental measurement in education. Using IQ tests for predicting recidivism in the criminal justice system, studying the impact of nutrition on cognitive development, and other such interests will continue to preoccupy those involved in mental measurement. Of course, any use of mental measurement should be justified on the basis of its contribution to improving the human condition.

By looking at education, certain principles can be illuminated, some of which can be applied to many other areas of use of mental measurement.

Telephone numbers at least represent some kind of idea: they are all addressed like codes for the central office to respond to. Implicit in the process of averaging is the process of adding. To obtain an average, first add a number of quantitative measures then divide by however many there are. This (all very simple) provided the quantities can be added, but for the most part with disparate subjects, they cannot be (Zacharias 1977, 69–70).

One of the interesting things to me is that these types of issues seldom if ever receive serious attention in published work in psychometrics. Rather, the professional conversation is usually confined to safe ground, that is, to the mathematics of statistical procedures or to the formal properties of a research design. But Zacharias and others raise the fundamental issue about the nature and quality of the data purportedly being measured. Psychometric "science" assumes but does not demonstrate the quality of the database that is being processed.

As with the case of Zacharias, opinions of linguists such as Roger Shuy (1977) get little or no response from the psychometric community. Yet he, like Zacharias, deals scientifically with the fundamentals of the nature of the phenomenon being measured—the quality of the database. In his classic article, Shuy makes the point, the profound point, that the most important part of language is its deep structure or deep meaning, its functional semantics. Its surface structure, that is its phonology and vocabulary, can be quantified very easily. However, Shuy argues that the part that interests the psychologist most, the semantics, are from the point of view of a linguist, least susceptible to measurement by traditional tests.

I suspect that the views of the physicist and the linguist are too hot to handle for the psychometrists who attempt to measure the mind. I am unaware of any recognition of these difficulties in the applied mental measurement literature. I might add that it is in precisely, these two areas of concern that we find the source of what some refer to as cultural bias in the IQ test. But it is really a validity problem, not mainly a bias or fairness problem.

In 1989, a summit conference was held on the construct of intelligence and its measurement in Melbourne, Australia. A set of selected papers from that conference was published in 1991 (Rowe 1991). Helga Rowe was principal research officer for the Australian Council for Educational Research. To the best of my knowledge, this was the most recent summit to attempt to make a state-of-the-art statement about the measurement of intelligence. Psychologists from fourteen countries were represented at the seminar, and the conference was used as a satellite conference preceding the Twenty-Fourth International Congress of Psychology which took place in Sydney, Australia.

Several important points appear in the conference papers. First, the importance of context in mental measurement was recognized.

Erickson's (1984) overview of research from an anthropological view shows, for example, that mental abilities (including language and mathematical abilities) that were once thought to be relatively or even totally (as presumed by classical learning theory and Piaget developmental theory) independent of context are much more sensitive to context than traditionally thought cognitive processes such as reasoning and understanding develop in the context of personal use and purpose. The demand characteristics of a learning task can be changed by altering the context within which it is presented (Rowe 1991, 6).

This fundamental matter of context makes measurement matters messy. It raises the number of variables to be considered exponentially. To recognize context is to complicate the task of the psychometrist astronomically. It is time for measurement scientists to stop sweeping such difficulties under the rug. Rowe (1991) goes on.

As pointed out by Erickson (1984), differences in performance as described earlier, cannot be explained merely in relation to abstract versus concrete thinking, as has been quite generally assumed. Rather, the differences in performance are very much related to differences in problem definition by self and others. When a person has made the problem his own, i.e., when he/she has formulated a task or question, he/she goes through a series of cognitive processes including decision-making points, each involving personal abilities, knowledge, and skills, as well as processes of social interaction that do not come into play when, for example, he/she is engaged in completing a worksheet or doing an IQ test. It is not just that learning tests are often "out of context" as Brickson notes, but they are in a context in which the power relationships and processes of social interaction are such that the student has no influence on problem formulation and the tasks offer no context of personal use and purpose.

A full appreciation of the role of context, personal purpose and use, and of processes of social interaction would fundamentally reshape our conceptualizations of and approaches to assessment, as well as to teaching and learning (Rowe 1991, 7).

Like the measurement perspective of the physicist Zacharias and the linguistic perspectives of the linguist Shuy, this issue of context raises another point that psychometric scientists have yet to address. The points are not trivial, but the responses to them have been, if we look at applied mental measurement in education today.

A second interesting point that came out of the Melbourne conference was that psychologists have no common definition of or theory of intelligence.

Although scientific psychologists have been studying intelligence for a century, they do not seem to have come closer to a widely acceptable, consistent general theory of intelligence. On the contrary, they offer an array of limited, although usually sophisticated subtheories, addressing specific issues with little concern for integration with other views (Richele 1991).

Finally, the Melbourne seminar on intelligence revealed several places where researchers failed to find the expected correlation between IQ and achievement in complex problem solving.

As can be seen in table 13.1, the overall results failed to fulfill the expectation of a close positive relationship of intelligence test scores and performance scores derived from system control. The reported correlation coefficients are remarkably low; in most cases, they are close to zero. Few coefficients reach values of 4. Only in four studies can correlation coefficients of this size be found. Thus, the reported results from these studies do not support the general assumption that intelligence tests are good predictors of an individual's performance when operating a complex system. In addition, most studies agree with respect to the interpretation of the results in two important ways. One, it is argued that the tasks (i.e., simulated systems) have higher ecological validity and are closer to reality than problem situations, such as intelligence tests' items or the Tower of Hanoi which have traditionally been studied by cognitive psychologists. Two, the low correlation coefficients allow us to infer that intelligence test scores cannot be regarded as valid predictors for problem solving and decision making in complex, real-life environments (Kluwe, Misiak, and Haider 1991, 228, 232).

Once again, these are not trivial issues, but the response to them has been trivial if we look at common practice in the schools.

To summarize, there are several nontrivial, interrelated, and overlapping measurement issues and problems that bear on the construct validity and the measurement validity of intelligence.

To fail to deal aggressively with these issues is to reduce the measurement of intelligence activities to little more than a meaningless ritual.

Applying intelligence and its measurement in schools

When it comes to the schools, the debate over the technical and scientific issues in mental measurement are of peripheral interest. However, when mental measurement is applied in the schools, then the value of that activity for school improvement must be examined. It can be seen from the quotations at the beginning of this article, quotations that come from the National Academy of Science panel report on placing children in special education, that the school use of tests calls for tests that assist in the design of instruction that results in benefits to students. By linking the activities in mental measurement to school treatment strategies and by linking both of those to student outcomes, and in particular beneficial outcomes, the traditional task and goal of mental measurement must be transformed. Initially, traditionally, and presently in the United States, the goal of mental measurement was and is merely ranking and classification to predict achievement (Hilliard 1990).

So the matter of requiring that professional activity be beneficial to students is the most important conceptual or paradigmatic change in American education as far as the use of intellectual assessment is concerned.

By requiring the benefits criterion, a whole new range of research studies is called for—true validity studies, instructional validity studies. How can validity studies that ignore variation in school treatment, failing to control for it, be considered scientifically valid (Kozol 1991)? If mental measurement, on the other hand, is to be used for diagnosis and remediation, how can validity be determined in ignorance of the reliability, validity, and quality control of the instructional practices, regular and "special"? Do children benefit from the uses of psychological services, especially the measurement of IQ? At the same time, do children benefit from special teaching services that are dictated by the results of tests? Are the services to which students are sentenced special pedagogically? The answers to each of these questions seem to be a resounding "no" (Glass 1983, Hehir and Latus 1993, Heller et al. 1982, Skyrtic 1991). In other words, the record on instructional benefits to students as a consequence of the use of mental measurement is abysmal.

Two points have not yet been considered in looking at the benefits question. First, we find that when good teaching is offered to children, many of whom fall into traditionally low-performing categories. Their "intellectual disabilities" appear to disappear (Backler and Eakin 1993, Edmonds 1979, and Sizemore 1988). In other words, there are children in schools whose grades and IQ test scores have been low, traditionally, who live in impoverished and even violent neighborhoods with all the things that are supposed to make learning difficult but who are some of the highest academic performers in their school districts or even in their states. Perhaps IQ predicts the quality of school treatment that children are likely to receive.

If a school such as the Vann school in Pittsburgh, the Madison school in Pittsburgh, or the Martinez school in Dallas is serving a population of students that would be expected to fall in the lower academic achievement quartile but their actual performance places them in the highest academic quartile, then the IQ correlation is a failure. IQ did not predict such achievement. Yet we find precisely that in many cases. But we really only need to find it in one case to show that the IQ tests predict future achievement if teaching service quality is not equalized as a part of the context within which children operate. Mental measurement and intelligence theorists have yet to do the types of validity studies to prove or disprove this. A rare exception may be found (Fuller 1977).

Second, we must ask the question, "Is mental measurement in the schools a prerequisite to the production of successful achievement with children?" I have been seeking out high-performing schools and teachers for the better part of three decades now. One of the things that is striking to me is that in excellent schools, there are almost no cases where the use of IQ or other means of making estimates of the mental capacities of students is an important part of the considerations for the design of instruction in these excellent schools nor does IQ inform instructional design for successful teachers! The highest performing educators work without the IQ net! Conversely, IQ teachers and IQ schools have nothing to brag about.

It ought to be clear to virtually anyone who looks at this problem that the current IQ ritual is irrelevant to the design of powerful, successful instruction for students, or that if mental measurement or assessment is to become useful in the school experience, then a paradigm shift is needed.

Fortunately, such a paradigm shift has already occurred among many psychologists and educators who are attempting to apply the work of cognitive change psychologists (Dent 1991; Feuerstein 1979, 1980; Feuerstein, Klein, and Tannenbaum 1991; Hehir and Latus 1993; Hilliard 1987a, 1987b; M. R. Jensen 1992; Lidz 1991).

To summarize, at the moment, psychology has yet to demonstrate its ability to measure the capacity of any children, let alone the capacity of children who are situated in different cultural and low socioeconomic contexts, using the medium of a standard language and cultural material in a set of pluralistic cultural contexts. Second, psychometrics cannot be developed by quantifying things that are not quantifiable. Third, IQ psychometry cannot validate the treatment categories to which mental measurement sentences schoolchildren, for example, the "educable mentally retarded" category and the "learning disabilities" category. Moreover, even if it could, educators have no unique, validated differentiated pedagogy for such categories. Fourth, there is a large database on effective schools that makes no reference whatsoever to mental measurement of intelligence, and there is a smaller database on highly effective schools also without mental measurements. Therefore, the mental measurement of intelligence is in no way a prerequisite for present success in school. No body of data shows that any use of traditional IQ or mental measurement is tied to valid teaching and learning. Therefore, IQ measurement is a professionally meaningless ritual. A ritual with unnecessarily harmful consequences that shapes professional thought and action in a negative way, causing professionals to overlook successful strategies and approaches in education. It is a ritual that shapes student self-image in a negative way.

The consequences of invalid theory and practice

It is almost scandalous that professionals in psychology today who serve the children of all the people have bought into the IQ myth. Unhappily, Arthur Jensen (1969, 1980) is not alone among psychologists, for example, who believe in the genetic inferiority of people of African descent when compared to Europeans. Snyderman and Rothman (1990) report on their survey of psychologists and researchers, many of whom are diplomates in their respective professional associations, such as some of the members of the American Psychological Association.

In this case, a plurality of experts (45 percent) and a majority of respondents believed the black-white IQ difference to be the product of both genetic and environmental variation, compared to only 15 percent who feel the difference is entirely due to environmental variation. The 24 percent of experts do not believe there are sufficient data to support any reasonable opinion, and 14 percent did not respond to the question. Eight of the experts (1 percent) indicate a belief in an entirely genetic determination. That a majority of experts who respond to this question believe genetic determinants to be important in the black-white IQ difference is remarkable in light of the overwhelmingly negative reaction from both the academic and public spheres that met Jensen's statement of the same hypothesis. Either expert opinion has changed dramatically since 1969, or the psychological and educational communities are not making their opinions known to the general public (Snyderman and Rothman 1990, 128–129).

Clearly, there is a need to explore the impact of such beliefs on the helping behavior of professionals, which parallel very closely the beliefs of the general public (Duke 1991). A well-documented, clear history of gross abuse exists here (Gould 1981, Guthrie 1976, Kamin 1974). Where we can see that there is no database to support the idea that mental measurement is helpful, such opinions raise the question of whether mental measurement is harmful. That is a question to which serious attention of researchers must be turned. The only justification for using IQ routinely, or for employing a system dependent on IQ, is that clear and substantial benefits (academic achievement benefits) accrue to students. It is not a good argument to say that IQ testing helps to get resources when neither the IQ test nor the help that the resources bring are beneficial.

The poverty of psychometric science is revealed when we note that there is no scientific definition of the variable "race" (Fairchild 1991, Montagu 1974, Yee 1983). There is no scientific accounting for the intervening variable of school "treatment." There is no scientific accounting for linguistic and cultural diversity in the design of measuring instruments (Helms 1992). But psychometricians are supremely confident of their measurement and of the predictive validity of their instruments.

The promise of intelligence thinking

Research in mental measurement can continue. Research in the utility of mental measurement can continue. But what good is intelligence if it does not help us to change instruction? Like thousands of others, I am deeply impressed with some of the advances in the study of the human mind and how it works. I am impressed with Jean Piaget, Milton Budoff, Robert Sternberg, Reuven Feuerstein, and Mogens Jensen (1992). I am impressed with the work of Howard Gardner (1983). They and others have given us a language that clarifies the workings of the human mind that highlights its dynamism, its growth as an open system, and the variety of ways in which the human mind can express itself, sometimes referred to as "multiple intelligences." But all of these advances in thinking will come to naught if the fundamental paradigm that brought us here is not revised.

I see people take the work of psychologists like Feuerstein, whose interest is in cognitive functions and structures and instead of looking at the power of the approach to produce changes in learners, become interested in how to score the assessment system and how to compare students to each other in a system that does not have ranking as its goal. I am interested too in the treatment of Gardner's (1983) work where many people who come to it with the old paradigm bring with them an interest in scoring multiple intelligences so that individuals may be ranked in multiple ways rather than one, losing, in my opinion, the potential of the construct change. Gardner's construct change enlarges the vision of educators about the variety in intellectual processes. It implies the need to address a broader range of curriculum goals. But the construct change is not accompanied by a paradigm shift. We may wind up with seven ways to hurt children rather than one. The essence of the paradigm shift is that we view the human intelligence as modifiable, as growing. That is just as true of the "seven intelligences" as it is of the one (Suzuki 1984). Sorting people into the new categories and ranking them within the categories will be as meaningless pedagogically as using one dimensional intelligence. On the other hand, the multiple intelligence map opens up the mind of the teachers to targets for mediation to enhance potential and to enrich curriculum.

I want to make it clear that I do not oppose research and the attempt to define intelligence and to measure it systematically. What I do oppose is acting as if those tasks have already been completed. I do not oppose attempting to use what is learned from the study of how the human mind functions to improve the education process. What I do oppose is acting as if non-pedagogically trained psychologists and non-instructionally related mental measurement devices have a meaningful and beneficial application to the design of effective instruction for students. I believe that the inertia in traditional practice prevents psychologists from putting their best foot forward.

I have often said that there is another paradigm for conceptualizing and assessing mental functions, a paradigm which has already been shown to be useful in improving the instructional process. This means that there is a meaningful function for psychologists in the educational process, a function which includes assessment, if not measurement, at this time, but a function which requires a fundamental change in the role of psychologists. In fact, to be prepared to perform a meaningful assessment, psychologists must become master teachers (Feuerstein 1980, M. R. Jensen 1992). It is through the application of teaching, of somewhat known validity, that learners can be provoked to reveal the patterns of thinking and learning that can be used to construct educational dialogue that can result in cognitive, affective, and content benefits for students.

I am willing to leave the door open; perhaps the future will yield a traditional test or assessment of intelligence and a consensus on the construct to benefit students. Should the benefits be clear and unmistakable? I shall be the first to embrace such an approach. However, my experience as a teacher and my understanding of the goals of psychometrics leaves me pessimistic about these possibilities—the fundamental issue being whether the mind is fixed and limited or modifiable and susceptible to growth through nurturing. Depending on our beliefs on this issue and our beliefs about the efficacy of instruction, we embark on one of two paradigmatic paths that diverge at an ever-growing rate.

Models of mental functioning, such as those proposed by the cognitive modifiability psychologists and by the multiple intelligence psychologists, are useful less because they answer the question of how to measure intelligence. But by conceiving of intelligence in the way that they do, they imply a pedagogical map that has vast implications for teacher training, assessment approaches, and approaches to the evaluation of achievement outcomes. For example, Gardner's (1983) map of multiple intelligences is less interesting to me as a device for classifying people among the intelligences than it is to establish the rich domain of human functioning toward which educational facilitation can be directed for all learners.

I believe that we have been stuck in the old paradigm because of politics, not because of professionalism. The activity of psychologists in ranking and classifying ethnic populations, who are deemed "racial" populations, is a blot on the history of the profession with a stain that clouds professional perception even to the present day. Psychology is, or ought to be, a healing discipline; if not, then not only does the construct of intelligence and the measurement of intelligence become irrelevant but psychology itself perhaps ought not exist. Happily, the model of what we could become and what we ought to become already exists. The kind of intelligence in the healing paradigm may someday be fully articulated and, yes, even measured.

Certainly, we want to assess the mind in valid and appropriate ways and to use the information from that assessment to create a better life for the people. But the beneficial aspects will not come about automatically, and until such time as they do come about, why bother to apply what we know about intelligence? Just stay in the laboratory until there is something beneficial to offer.

CHAPTER 4

Racial and Ethnic Bias in Test Construction

Donald Ross Green

(Reprinted here with the explicit permission of the author)

Statement of the problem

The standardized achievement tests used in schools are often said to be biased against and thus inappropriate for children belonging to disadvantaged racial and ethnic minorities. If this is so, then there are two possible sources of such bias. The first may originate in the preconceptions and thought patterns of the test item writers. The second may result from the customary item tryout and selection procedures used in test construction. This second possible source of bias is the general topic investigated in this study.

A number of problems occurred when trying to consider bias in achievement tests because the criteria of bias are not completely clear. When most recent writers (Cardall and Coffman 1964, Potthoff 1966, Cleary and Hilton 1968, Messick and Anderson 1970, Green 1971) speak of bias, they say something about tests which measure different things when used with different groups. How might item tryout and selection procedures produce such a result?

The typical procedure in building standardized achievement and aptitude tests has remained essentially unchanged over many years (cf. Lord and Novick 1968, Chapter 15; Ruch 1929, Chapter 2). The first step is to develop a pool of items meeting various specifications as to form and content. Next, these items are given to a sample of individuals—the step in question here. Various item statistics, such as point biserial correlation's (item versus total score), are calculated, and the "best" items are then chosen. "Best" is customarily characterized first and foremost by a high relationship of the item to the total score. Other characteristics such as difficulty and the effectiveness of distracters (in multiple-choice tests) are also considered. Most of these latter item characteristics are related to the item-test correlation to some degree. Therefore, the items which "discriminate" best (i.e., show the highest relationship to total score) are the ones usually chosen. This in turn means that the characteristics or attributes of the individuals in the tryout sample which are most responsible for differences in total score determine which items tend to be chosen and determine, in effect, what the test measures within the range of possibilities available in the item pool. That is to deal with the items, the individuals tested call upon certain qualities, attitudes, knowledge, or skills found in widely varying degrees in their group. The items most sensitive to these attributes of the tryout sample then get selected.

Consequently, the possibility exists that the items selected are biased and discriminate against groups unlike the modal group in the tryout sample. If some atypical group has traits not prominent in the tryout sample and if these traits interact more strongly with the items than do the attributes the group shares with the majority, then the tests will measure the distinctive characteristics of this group rather than the trait or traits measured in the more typical groups. Another possibility is that the atypical group is uniformly low on the measured traits but not on other equally relevant but unmeasured attributes. In either of these cases, one could say the resulting test is biased. In the first instance, it is biased because it measures different things for different groups unbeknownst to the users; in the second instance, it measures only a portion of the relevant behaviors but is taken to measure them all.

Given circumstances such as those just described, then the use of eleven "average" item tryout samples will result in the selection of item sets unsuited to one or more of the various racial, ethnic, cultural minority groups in our schools. From this, it may follow that the use of a single tryout group can never solve the problem—perhaps only the construction of separate tests would do so although the solution would have obvious drawbacks. Another alternative might be to use the same test but different items weights for different groups.

The need to consider such unattractive possibilities depends on how strongly the nature of a tryout sample determines the outcome of item selection. It is customarily assumed that the choice of people for item tryouts does not have much effect on the item selection although eleven "atypical" groups (such as disadvantaged children) are usually avoided. This amounts to the assumption that the test items function much the same way with all kinds of people. Some evidence for evaluating this assumption is presented in this report.

Related literature

Prior work on test bias does not seem to have dealt directly with these item tryout and selection procedures. In fact, as far as achievement tests are concerned, very little work of any sort on the matter of bias appears to be available. The work on bias in intelligence and aptitude tests is more extensive, but aspects of the bias issue other than the one considered here have dominated discussions.

That children's intelligence test scores are related to their social and economic status was reported by Binet and others more than sixty years ago and has been studied and argued about ever since. For a long time, these debates largely stayed within the bounds of the much older and highly emotional nature-nurture controversy perhaps because many felt that the then new tests could settle the issue (Terman 1916, 1920). Since the intensity of the arguments shows no sign of diminishing after fifty years (consider, for example, the response to Jensen 1969), that hope may be considered unreasonable. In any case, the test score differences favoring the more privileged elements of society remain a fact (Coleman et al. 1966). It may be added that the accusations of the misuse and the misinterpretation of scores (Hunter and Rogers 1967, Mercer 1971) are also factual in some, if not most, instances.

However, the issue here is the nature of the tests themselves. This has not been as widely studied as it might be. Apparently, the first serious attempt to examine test items for bias was led by Allison Davis and his colleagues twenty years ago (Eells et al. 1951). They examined several existing group intelligence tests and the items in them in an attempt to determine the factors built into the test which are related to differences in performance between cultural groups. They concluded: "Variations in opportunity for familiar cultural words, objects, or processes required for answering the test items seem…the most adequate general explanation" (Eells 1951, 68). This sort of objection is also often made in achievement tests (Wasserman 1969) but is not a valid basis for asserting bias in an achievement test unless the missing knowledge is irrelevant to what is being measured. Consider the finding reported by Chang and Raths (1971) that achievement test items which discriminate between middle- and lower-class groups reflect a different curricular emphasis on the part of the teachers. This is more nearly teacher-bias than test bias. In an ability test, such objections have direct logical merit.

Interestingly, the subjects in the Eells study were all white and drawn from the schools of "a western industrial city of about one hundred thousand people." One result of the study was the publication of the Davis-Eells Games (1953) which was designed to eliminate this kind of cultural bias. Three things may be noted about the test, which is now out of print. First, the test proved to yield differences between middle and low socioeconomic status (SES) groups (Angelino and Shedd 1955) as substantial as those found using other group intelligence tests. Second, Davis and Eells eliminated the items that showed SES differences in difficulty only if they could rationalize the differences as a consequence of opportunity. Lastly, they apparently did not look at the differences between SES groups with respect to item discrimination. The common interpretation of the outcome of the Davis-Eells test and similar efforts by others has been that the task of building a "culture-free" or "culture-fair" test may be not only impossible but inappropriate because such a test would not be valid as a measure of general ability, as indeed was the case for the Davis-Eells Games (Lorge 1966).

Supporting this view is work such as that of Lesser, Fifer, and Clark (1965). This study showed that patterns of ability are different for different ethnic groups. It also showed that within any one ethnic group, quantitative differences resulted from socioeconomic status, but the patterns for SES groups were very similar. That is, the lower-class and middle-class groups of any one ethnic group had similar patterns, but the latter had higher scores. Such data imply that any test measuring several abilities—as most ability and achievement tests do—is automatically stacking the cards against one ethnic group or another.

Furthermore, Williams (1970) reports that he has built a test biased in favor of blacks. His validation studies of the instrument as a measure of academic aptitude are not yet complete, but if Williams can produce a valid ability test favoring blacks, then it is probable that most ability tests are biased. In the meantime, many people are taking this to be established fact and assertions that group intelligence tests necessarily discriminate against various minority and disadvantaged groups in our society have been increasing in number and vehemence. Some school systems (New York City, for example) have virtually abandoned the use of such tests (Gilbert 1966). Similarly, some college personnel now argue that the various placement and ability tests traditionally used are inappropriate (Brown and Russell 1964).

Many of the assertions made about bias in ability tests appear to be sound, but, as Anastasi (1968) has pointed out, bias in prediction involves a distinct set of issues. None of the preceding considerations necessarily apply if the test in question is meant to be used as a predictor of some criterion performance. For example, if one defines bias as systematic underprediction, then the attacks on the aptitude tests used for college admissions appear largely unfounded. The claim that such tests fail to function among disadvantaged minority students in the way they do in other groups lacks supporting evidence. A series of studies at both the high school and college levels show that academic aptitude tests frequently predict grades just as well for minority groups as they do for more privileged groups. Only the work of Green and Farquhar (1965) points to a different conclusion among a half dozen or so studies on the issue. In fact, some tests appear to overpredict the performance of lower-class and Negro students in contrast to middle-class and white students (Hewer 1965, Stanley and Porter 1967, Cleary 1968, Davis and Temp 1971).

Even in this relatively well explored area, much remains to be done, such as finding ways to deal with the possibility of bias in the criterion measure (Linn and Werts 1971). In addition, there is often more than one reasonable definition of bias in criterion-related validity situations (Thorndike 1971, Darlington 1971). As Potthoff (1966) has pointed out, the operational demonstration of bias is even more difficult and ambiguous when test validity cannot be defined as the relationship of scores to a directly measurable criterion. Any test yielding scores meant to be an indication of status—be it in achievement, in intelligence, or in what have you—creates such problems.

One approach consistent with the definition of bias offered at the start of this paper is to examine the items rather than the whole test for bias. Here, bias may be defined as an item by group interaction. Three studies (Cardall and Coffman 1964, Cleary and Hilton 1968, Angoff and Ford 1971) using this approach have been reported.

They each found statistically significant item by race interactions in the College Entrance Examination Board aptitude tests which they used (EAT and PSAT). Nevertheless, Cleary and Hilton concluded that "the PSAT is not biased for practical purposes" while Angoff and Ford suggested the "interaction was simply the difference in performance levels on the test shown by the two races." These studies were based largely upon a consideration of item difficulties.

Item interrelationships are also a relevant consideration. Data obtained by Kennedy et al. (1963) show that the grandfather of them all, the Stanford-Binet (Terman and Merrill 1960), produced equal or higher itemtest correlation for an all-black southern sample than was reported in either the 1937 or the 1960 standardization. Also, Merz (1970) has reported that the factor structure of the Goodenough-Harris Drawing Test is substantially the same for samples of black, white, Mexican, and Anglo children in the southwest.

Incomplete as this research on bias in ability tests may be, it is way ahead of that on bias in achievement tests which is essentially nonexistent. The claims of bias in achievement tests (Wasserman 1969, Williams 1970, Houston 1971) need investigation. The approach of item by group interactions seems to be the logical place to begin. Certainly, it seems reasonable to believe that a test based on items selected for a particular group (such as inner city black children) would be less biased against them and therefore more useful for them.

Objectives of the study

To explore such a possibility, this study compares the results of using three disadvantaged minority groups—northern, urban black; southern, rural black; and southwestern Mexican American—as tryout samples in contrast to white, advantaged groups in the same regions.

The study attempts to determine whether or not an item tryout using these different groups would lead to the selection of different items from the item pool and, if so:

1. Do the different items selected measure different things?
2. Are the resulting item sets "better" for the minority groups in the sense that they are more reliable and have better functioning items (higher point biserial correlations)?
3. Will the relative discrepancy in scores favoring majority groups be reduced by using a minority tryout group?

Limitations of the study

The major limitation of this study is the restricted nature of the item pool: all items come from an already published test. They are, therefore, preselected and may be limited in their possibility of eliciting differential reactions from the sample groups. Also, it should be noted that grade and test level are not independent; the test levels were designed to be continuous and to articulate well, but they are different tests. Thus, the assumption made throughout the following material that grade differences are meaningful may not be justified. Finally, because of limitations of time and money, not all relevant analyses of data could be made.

Method

The basis data for this study were derived from that obtained during the standardization of the California Achievement Tests 1970 edition (CAT-70) published by CTB/McGraw-Hill. The CAT-70 is a general achievement battery with five overlapping levels. It was designed to measure educational attainment and to provide an analysis of learning difficulties. It is basically similar to the 1957 edition and generally measures:

1. the ability to understand the meaning of the content material presented;
2. the performance of the student in applying rules, facts, concepts, conventions, and principles to solve problems in the basic curricular material; and
3. the level of performance of the student in using the tools of reading, mathematics, and language in progressively more complicated situations.

The tests in the battery which were investigated in this study are Reading Vocabulary, Reading Comprehension, Total Reading, Mathematics Computation, Mathematics Concepts and Problems,

Total Mathematics, Language Mechanics, Language Usage and Structure, and Total Language. Total Reading, Total mathematics, and Total Language were treated as tests separate from their parts. The standardization took place early in 1970 and involved over 200,000 students in about 400 schools. Then sampling design called for obtaining a sample of school districts stratified by region (seven areas), school district size (three categories by average enrollment per grade), community type (urban town, rural, other), and control (public or parochial). Within the districts, schools were chosen randomly for each test level, and all students in the selected schools who were in appropriate grades took the test.

The items in the battery came from a variety of sources, but it is fair to say that they were written by and for "middle America." The tryout samples also fit the description. Thus, the test should favor white, middle-class Americans if they favor any group.

Sample

All schools participating in the CAT-70 standardization answered questionnaires which provided information on the basic character of the area served (e.g., residential suburb, inner part of a large city, etc.), the percentage of white students, the percentage of children from homes where another language is spoken, and the percentage of children in families falling in each of four SES groups defined by parental occupation (professional-managerial, white collar, skilled, unskilled).

From the data on these questionnaires, seven groups of schools were drawn for the study. The characteristics and sizes of these groups are shown in table 1. The samples used in the study are drawn from schools serving pupils highly homogeneous with respect to ethnic background and rather homogeneous with respect to socioeconomic status. Only at Grade 10 was it not possible always to find schools meeting these criteria in the standardization population; sufficiently segregated tenth grades were found only in the South.

The groups were paired for comparisons as follows:

1. Northern, black, central city versus Northern, white suburban (II versus I)
2. Southern, black, rural versus Southern, white, suburban (IV versus III)
3. Southern, black rural versus Southern, white, rural (IV versus V)
4. Southwestern, Mexican American versus Southwestern, Anglo-American, suburban (VI versus VII)

Table 1

CHARACTERISTICS OF THE SAMPLE GROUPS

Group Number	Geographic Region	Residential Type	Ethnic Group	Socioeconomic Status	Number of Cases by Grade				
					1	3	5	8	10
	North	Residential Suburban	White (97%)'	High (81%)'	299	225	265	328	
II	North	Central City	Black (99%)	Low (81%)	285	304	278	250	
III	South	Residential Suburban	White (99%)	High (77%)	361	211	293	304	279
IV	South	Rural	Black (100%)	Low (96%)	202	220	171	245	183
V	South	Rural	White (91%)	Low (81%)	323	200	199	296	246
VI	Southwest	Small and Large Cities	Mexican-American (87%)	Low (82%)	146	144	169	399	
VII	Southwest	City and Suburban	Anglo-American (99%)	High (81%)	189	218	249	277	

The states containing these particular school systems are North: Illinois, Indiana, Kansas, New Jersey; South: Alabama, Georgia, South Carolina; and Southwest: Arizona, Oklahoma, Texas. Estimated percent of cases falling in the category. The 81 percent speak mostly Spanish at home.

Enough schools meeting the appropriate criteria to provide between 150 and 300 students for each group at each of five grade levels were selected. Each of the grade levels (1, 3, 5, 8, and 10) corresponds to a different level of the CAT-70 battery.

Grade 10 comparisons were made in the South only. No analyses were made of the total language scores in Grades 1, 5, and 8 for the Northern, white group and in Grades 1 and 8 for the Northern, black group. Therefore, of the 315 possible analyses (7 groups × 9 tests × 5 grades), only 274 separate analyses were made.

Data analyses

The basic procedure used for examining the data was an item selection routine. Each of the seven groups was treated as a tryout sample with the items in each test functioning as an item pool. For each group on each test at each grade, the "best" half of the items (i.e., those with the highest item-test correlations) were noted. Four kinds of analyses were made:

1. The number and percent of items chosen for one group in the pair but not for the other was recorded. These were labeled "biased." The number of these biased items in any one comparison indicates the degree to which the two groups were compared in this way; the remaining analyses were made only for the four pairs listed previously.

2. Scores for each group in a pair were obtained on both sets of biased items. These two tests may be called the "majority biased test" and the "minority biased test" since they contain the items uniquely best for the respective groups. The correlation between each group's score on the two tests was found. From these correlations, estimates of the variance not common to the two biased item tests were made to judge how different the sets of items really are in what they measure. Thus, this analysis supplements the first.

3. Another analysis consisted of examining and comparing full-test and half-test KR 20 reliability estimates since differential reliability would be a form of bias indicating that

the test scores have a larger error component in one group than they do in another group.

4. Finally, mean scores on the full-test, the half-test, and the biased item tests were examined for changes in relative status of the groups as a result of item selection.

Table 2

PROPORTIONS OF BIASED ITEMS FOR COMPARISON GROUPS BY GRADE AND TEST

Test	Number of Items Selected	Comparison Groups			
		II vs. I	IV vs. III	IV vs V	VI vs VII
Grade 1					
Vocabulary	46	.41	.33	.35	.59
Comprehension	12	.25	.58	.33	.42
Total Reading	58	.40	.36	.34	.69
Computation	20	.15	.25	.40	.25
Concepts & Problems	24	.42	.38	.42	.58
Total Mathematics	44	.16	.25	.23	.41
Mechanics	19	.42	.21	.21	.58
Usage & Structure	10	.30	.30	.40	.40
Total Language	39		.24	.27	.54
Grade3					
Vocabulary	20	.30	.65	.35	.45
Comprehension	23	.22	.26	.22	.35
Total Reading	43	.28	.42	.28	.33
Computation	36	.17	.28	.22	.25
Concepts & Problems	23	.35	.48	.35	.43
Total Mathematics	59	.29	.32	.30	.32
Mechanics	33	.48	.42	.30	.45
Usage & Structure	13	.31	.46	.23	.46
Total Language	46	.41	.30	.28	.48
Grade 5					
Vocabulary	20	.50	.55	.35	.70
Comprehension	21	.48	.43	.29	.52
Total Reading	41	.46	.46	.37	.61
Computation	34	.41	.38	.21	.41
Concepts & Problems	20	.50	.40	.20	.55
Total Mathematics	54	.44	.46	.20	.46
Mechanics	40	.45	.35	.25	.53
Usage & Structure	21	.33	.48	.38	.33
Total Language	61		.30	.16	.26
Grades					
Vocabulary	20	.40	.15	.15	.45
Comprehension	23	.22	.39	.30	.39
Total Reading	43	.26	.23	.21	.44
Computation	24	.25	.46	.29	.29
Concepts & Problems	25	.36	.40	.36	.28
Total Mathematics	49	.29	.49	.35	.29
Mechanics	36	.42	.33	.42	.39
Usage & Structure	25	.36	.56	.32	.16
Total Language	61		.15	.15	.18
Grade 10					
Vocabulary	20		.55	.40	
Comprehension	23		.22	.22	
Total Reading	43		.42	.30	
Computation	24		.33	.33	
Concepts & Problems	25		.40	.32	
Total Mathematics	49		.33	.24	
Mechanics	40		.38	.35	
Usage & Structure	27		.41	.30	
Total Language	67		.21	.19	
Median proportions for all tests and grades		.36	.38	.30	.43

Results

Proportions of biased items. The item selection routine yielded a series of tests "best" for each group, half as long as the original test when N was odd, the expression (N + 1)12 was used to determine the length of the half-test. The next step was to identify those items selected for only one of the two members of a pair—the so-called biased items. Obviously, the number of biased items has to be the same for each group in a pair. This number as a proportion of the items in each half-test is an index of the degree to which the item in each half-test is an index of the degree to which the item selection procedure produces a different test for the two groups.

Table 2 exhibits these proportions for the four basic comparison groups. The proportions do not appear to vary systematically by grade or test. However, certain groups appear considerably more like each other than are others by the criterion of the relative size of these proportions. It can be readily seen from table 2 that the differences between the Mexican American and Anglo groups tend to be larger than those between the black and white pairs.

The medians of these proportions for all possible pairs are shown in table 3. The overall median proportion is approximately .30. As expected, the white, middle-class groups are consistently more like each other (these pairs have lower medians) than they are like the minority groups. The latter also have more in common than they share with the three majority groups. The Southern, rural, white group does not fully fit into this otherwise clear pattern; in general, they appear more like the three minority groups than they resemble the three suburban groups. Of course, economically they are undoubtedly more disadvantaged than the suburban groups albeit much less so than the Southern, black group.

Independence of biased item tests. All groups differ from their pairs to some degree by the criterion of proportions of biased items and some of the differences appear to be substantial. However, it is possible that these sets of biased items still measure much the same thing. To examine this possibility, scores for each individual were obtained on both biased item tests. This was possible since each individual answered all items. The correlations between these two scores were obtained for each group on each test. These correlations varied from −.17 to +.82 with a median of about .5 which leaves a lot of variance unaccounted for. Since the number of biased items was very small in many cases, the reliabilities of the biased tests are typically low. But even allowing for this, it appears that in many instances the majority and minority tests measure quite different things and as a rule do so for both groups involved.

Table 3

MEDIAN PROPORTIONS OF BIASED ITEMS
FOR EACH PAIR OF GROUPS

Group		II	III	IV	V	VI	VII
		.36	.26	.35	.30	.38	.26
II	.36		.33	.26	.25	.25	.41
III	.26	.33		.38	.30	.33	.27
IV	.35	.26	.38		.30	.30	.41
V	.30	.25	.30	.30		.24	.33
VI	.38	.25	.33	.30	.24		.43
VII	.26	.41	.27	.41	.33	.43	

Changes in test characteristics. A special case of bias occurs if the test scores of one group contain substantially more error than they do for another group. The overall median KR 20s on the full-tests for groups I through VII are .91, .91, .91, .92, .93, .90, and .92, respectively. Obviously, there is little evidence of bias by this criterion although a test-by-test comparison of these reliabilities shows that the figures are mostly higher for the majority group (97 of 162 comparisons). The data concerning half-test reliabilities also show a very small amount of bias.

The item-test correlations after item selection show only slight improvements and the uniformity of the increases prevents one from inferring the presence of substantial bias.

Changes in test scores. Another way to look at bias is to assert that the scores of some groups are unfairly low because the test does not adequately measure all the relevant abilities or knowledge and in particular does not measure well those relevant attributes on which the group in question happens to score well. If the item pool contains items which measure these attributes at all, a selection routine using this group might be expected to increase the importance of these attributes in determining the total score, thereby reducing the disadvantage of the group. Therefore, the three minority groups considered here might be expected to do relatively better on the items selected as best for them than they did on the original full-test. Each group's full- to half-test improvement on each of the nine tests in the battery was compared to the improvement shown by its comparison group. Table 4 reports the number of tests on which a group showed more full- to half-test improvement than was shown by its comparison group. The minority groups showed greater relative improvement consistently in the upper grades but not in Grades 1 and 3. As was the case for proportions of biased items, the Southern, rural, white group does not fit the pattern: the item selection procedure helped them as often as it helped the rural blacks perhaps because their initial scores were more alike to begin with, especially in the lower grades.

Table 4

**NUMBER OF TESTS ON WHICH EACH GROUP
SHOWED MORE FULL-TO HALF-TEST
MEAN SCORE GAIN THAN ITS COMPARISON GROUP**

| | Comparison Groups | | | | | | | | | |
Grade	11&1		IV & III		IV&V		VI&VII		Totals Min/Maj		X^2	p
	7	1b		8	0	9	7	2	15	20	0.7	NS
3	2	7	8	1	5	4	4	5	19	17	.01	NS
5	7	1b	8	1		8	8	1	24	11	4.8	.05
8	8	0b	6	3	7	2	6	3	27	8	10.3	.01
10			6	3	7	2			13	5	3.6	.10
Totals	24	9	29	16	20	25	25	11	98	61	8.6	.01
X^2	6.8		3.8		0.6		5.4		8.6			
p	.01		.05		NS		.02		.01			

•Let Y = majority group mean, X minority *910Lp* me n. nd let f and h represent
11-t st ang ha test, respectively. Then $Y, X, - 2(Y'' - X'') 0$ favors minority;
$Y, - X, - 2(-Y'' - X'') < 0$ favors majority.

Note that analyses were not made for the total language of the
CAT-70 for this group at this grade. Therefore, comparisons were
made for only eight tests.

Table 5

**NUMBER OF COMPARISONS IN WHICH MEAN DIFFERENCE
ON BIASED ITEM TEST
FAVORS EACH GROUP**

Grade	Comparison Groups								Totals Min/Maj		X^2	p
	11&1		IV & III		IV&V		VI & VII					
1	5	3'	6	3	8	1	8	1	27	8	10.3	.01
3	5	4	5	4	3	6	7	2	20	16	0.4	NS
5	7	1"	5	4	7	2	7	2	26	9	8.3	.01
8	8	0'	9	0	6	3	5	4	28	7	12.6	.001
10			6	3	5	4			11	7	0.9	NS
Totals	25	8	31	14	29	16	27	9	112	47		
X^2	8.8		6.4		3.8		9.0		26.6			
p	.01		.02		.05		.01		001			

et $\overline{M}$ = majority mean on majority test, X_m = minority mean on majority test, Y majority mean on minority test, and X = minority mean on minority test. Then $\overline{M}$ - X_m, $\overline{M}$ - Y, X favors minority - $\overline{M}$ - X_m, 0 - X favors majority.

The majority biased item tests are almost uniformly more difficult for both groups than are the minority biased item tests. In addition, the differences between majority group mean scores and minority group mean scores are usually smaller on the minority biased item tests than on the majority biased item tests. Table 5 shows the frequencies of this selection and the result tends to hold for all groups at all grades. The disadvantaged group is less disadvantaged when tested with items selected as uniquely best for them. In other words, the data show that the relative advantage of majority groups is reduced when using items chosen as best for the minority group but is increased when using items chosen as best for themselves.

Conclusions

The four analyses of the data described previously permit the following conclusions:

1. Different tryout samples lead to the selection of somewhat different sets of items. Considering the restriction on range and variety of points of view represented in the item pool, the 30 percent proportion of biased items, which was the average found in this study, seems large. That is, it seems likely that a majority of biased items would have been selected if the item pool had been more heterogeneous.

2. The more economically dissimilar the groups contrasted, the less likely it is that they will produce data leading to the selection of the same set of items.

3. If a biased test is a test that contains a substantial proportion of items that would not have been selected had they been tried on some other particular group, then probably most tests are biased against most groups.

4. By this criterion of bias, the tests used here are more biased against minority groups than against middle-class white children. This is probably true for most published batteries of standardized tests.

5. The proportion of biased items is a fairly good but uneven criterion of bias since in most cases, the biased item tests do measure different things. What is measured depends on which group is used for selection and which group is being tested. This conclusion is not uniformly true and varies widely according to test, grade, and tryout group.

6. The psychometric quality of the half-tests was only very slightly better than that of the originals. That is, the effect of the item selection procedure was small presumably because all the items were already a product of an item selection procedure and because the battery is rather homogeneous in style and point of view.

7. The half-tests were barely more reliable for the minority groups than for the majority groups, but this improvement is small in both kinds of groups and suggests minimal bias of this sort in the battery.

8. The use of items particularly suited to a tryout group will improve the chances of good scores among individuals from similar groups. The outcome may be more likely in the upper grades.

9. The amount of relative improvement scores that a minority group could expect to gain by using tests built with tryout groups like itself does not appear to be very large. The elative improvement is most unlikely to overcome any large discrepancy between typical scores in that group and those in more favored groups.

10. It should be possible to build tests somewhat biased in favor of any group by using a fair sample of that group for item selection data.

Recommendations and questions

The conclusions strongly suggest that there should be some changes and additions to the test construction procedures commonly used whenever there is a possibility that the resulting instrument will be used with people belonging to a group ethnically or culturally different from the test builder's principal reference group. Clearly, the first additional step is to obtain data on all relevant groups separately. It is important to note that if a set of items is likely to measure different attributes in different groups, the majority group in a tryout sample will determine which attributes are most strongly measured and the odds are that the inclusion of one or more minorities will merely obscure the issue. Just as the degree of minority representation in standardization samples can have only a small influence on norms, minority group presence in tryout samples dominated by some solid majority will not accomplish much.

What is needed is a way to (1) select unbiased items, (2) compensate for known bias by establishing alternate weighing and scoring schemes, (3) interpret scores according to the group membership of the examinee, or at least, and (4) acknowledge and document the existence of the bias and its effect on scores. Until more experience is available in using various kinds of separate tryout groups, it is not reasonable to state a preference among these options; a number of questions need to be answered first, such as:

1. What proportion of items tried can one expect to find "unbiased" by each of various criteria?
2. Can one expect simple scoring and weighing schemes to reduce bias?
3. Are the same criterion measures appropriate for all groups?
4. What sort of indices of bias could one offer that would be readily interpretable?

If the only favorable procedure turns out to be the last option, a test constructor could choose to build alternate versions, each biased toward a different group; the problems created by adopting this procedure are large and many but not necessarily insoluble.

In addition to exploration of the effects of variations in tryout groups, studies are needed on the role of points of view, cognitive style, and/or ethnic background among those contributing to the item pool. Would blacks tend to create items more useful for black children? Many blacks believe so. It seems obvious the Spanish-speaking item writers can produce better items for Spanish-speaking children than could someone who could not write in that language. Yet we still often use English language tests with children whose native language is not English and claim to be measuring something other than facility with English. It is, of course, less obvious if the children are fully bilingual. Are black children bilingual?

The answers to these and many other questions one might raise are not obvious. What is obvious is that it is no longer adequate for those who build tests to argue that bias is largely a matter of misuse or to say that they cannot see why a particular test would be biased and thus ignore the matter. All tests are not necessarily biased, but any test may be. Until there are good answers to these question, research on the matter should be a standard part of producing a test.

Acknowledgments

Special thanks are due to my colleague, Dr. George Burket, who first suggested this use of item selection procedures and who offered valuable advice throughout. I would also like to thank Dr. Joseph L. Dionne who gave encouragement and who ensured that CTB/McGraw-Hill provided the facilities and personnel needed at a cost substantially in excess of that provided by the grant. Finally, I would like to thank Lois Maclin who kept track of the entire project, made a number of statistical analyses, constructed all the tables, and edited the entire report.

CHAPTER 5

Alternative Methods for Assessing African Americans
Sharks in the Water

Harold E. Dent

Thank you, Dr. Thomas and Ms. Hunnicutt of the African American Studies Department of City College and Dr. Trotter of the Bay Area Association of Black Psychologists for putting together this symposium on IQ testing of African Americans, a subject which has occupied much of my time and energy for almost thirty years. Here we are in beautiful San Francisco in 1998 discussing the Larry P. case and the implementation, or lack thereof, of Judge Peckham's landmark decision to ban the use of IQ tests on African American students in California's public schools. Some critiques have claimed that this case actually started in 1968. That incorrect assumption was made because the Association of Black Psychologists (ABPsi) was born here in San Francisco in 1968 and one of the principal reasons for starting that organization at that time was the inappropriate use of biased psychological tests on African Americans in all aspects of their lives, education, employment, college admissions, etc. Actually, it wasn't until three years later, in November 1971, that the Larry P. case was officially filed in federal court.

When I became involved in this case, it was to help black parents who were concerned because their children had been wrongly placed in special education classes and without their knowledge. It was not my intention to devote thirty years of my professional life to the cause of challenging the bias in IQ testing.

We actually thought that by bringing this tragedy to the attention of the appropriate authorities, the problem would be easily resolved. After those efforts were unsuccessful, we thought that certainly the weight of a federal court decision which came in June of 1972 would settle the issues and our involvement would be ended. Then there were the appeals, two of them, one by the City of San Francisco and the other by the state of California. After each appeal was decided in our favor, we again assumed our involvement was complete. In effect, there were appeals after each victory and new cases filed challenging the appeal decisions. Now thirty years later, the California Department of Education (CDE) sets in place additional barriers to forestall full implementation of the IQ ban.

This scenario reminds me of the story of an old fisherman. As the story goes, there was an old man in a small fishing village who was too old to go out with the younger fishermen as he had for many years. But the village had experienced hard times because fishing was very bad, and for a long time, the fishing boats would come in empty-handed. So one day, the old man decided that he would venture out on his own. He was gone for a long time, but eventually, his experience and patience were rewarded. He felt a tremendous tug on his line. He wrestled tenaciously with the struggling fish and finally the fish was reeled in. The fish was too large for the weakened old man to haul into his little boat. So he tied it alongside his boat and started rowing the long way back to his village. As he rowed back, he thought that his catch would bring joy to the village and there would be much celebration. When he reached the harbor, many villagers were there waiting to greet him. But when they pulled the fish out of the water, much to their dismay, they found little more than a skeleton. On his way back to his village the sharks had nibbled and eaten so much of this fish that there was very little left. The moral of this story is that although you may be successful in achieving your goal, you must remember there are those who work to overturn your accomplishment. The sharks are out there.

There are lots of sharks in those waters!

Alternative assessment

When Dr. Thomas asked me to discuss the topic, Alternative Assessment, my first thought was to provide a sweeping synthesis of the popular approaches to assessment currently reported in the literature. Before searching the literature, I started to compile a list of different assessment models I knew of and soon realized that this would merely constitute an academic exercise which a beginning psychology student could easily accomplish in a relatively short time on the Internet, recognizing the state of the art of today's technology. [For those who wish to undertake such a task, the brief list of alternative assessment approaches which I quickly identified included: authentic assessment (Taylor 1992), cognitive assessment (Sternberg 1982), criterion assessment (Campbell 1992), curriculum-based assessment (Tucker 1985), dynamic assessment (Lidz 1987), interactive assessment (Haywood and Tzuriel 1991), nondiscriminatory assessment (Ysseldyke and Regan 1980), nondiscriminatory cognitive assessment (Figueroa 1984), performance assessment (Neill, Bursh, Shaeffer, Thall, Yohe, and Zappardino 1997), and realistic assessment (Dent 1996)]. I quickly abandoned that notion but was still faced with the task of preparing a presentation on Alternative Assessment that had particular application to the Larry P. case and the California dilemma.

Fortunately, Dr. Thomas came to my rescue. He called and said that he had just received a set of questions from the California Department of Education for the Intelligence Testing Advisory Panel concerning IQ testing. I first thought the ITAP was another new IQ test which I had not yet heard about. Or perhaps I had just misunderstood him and had rearranged the letters. I was familiar with the ITPA, the Illinois Test of Psycholinguistic Abilities. Dr. Thomas explained that the CDE had established a committee, the Intelligence

Testing Advisory Panel (ITAP), to advise the Special Education Division on the complex issue of IQ testing. The ITAP was charged with the task of advising the CDE on how to establish "a process and set of criteria to identify acceptable, non-biased intelligence tests."

Dr. Thomas asked me to include some comments about those question in my presentation. After reviewing the questions that Dr. Thomas faxed, it was apparent why he asked me to review and comment on those questions. I was extremely puzzled by these questions, and I suspect Dr. Thomas was also. I wondered why CDE, which had spent 30 years in litigation on the subject of bias in intelligence testing, would have to enlist the aid of an outside "panel of experts" to advise it on issues which Judge Peckham had explicitly defined in his 131-page Larry P. decision. The Peckham decision has been thoroughly discussed by experts in the field and cited in the special education literature more than any other legal decision in the last two decades.

After a careful review of the questions, it was apparent to me that the motivation of those in the CDE who composed the questions was something other than the identification of non-biased tests to determine the appropriate academic placement of African American children. If the department was sincere in its search for a procedure by which to identify non-biased tests of intelligence, it would seem to me there was a logical or reasonable way to approach the task internally before calling in outsiders. First, the department could have assigned its test specialists (if there are such specialists in the department) and/or legal staff to review the basis on which Judge Robert F. Peckham issued his landmark decision to conclude that standardized tests of intelligence were culturally biased against African American students. (If there are no such specialists in the CDE, who determines what tests the department requires local districts to use to assess student performance?) Judge Peckham was extremely explicit in his "findings of the court." In effect, Judge Peckham carefully identified the criteria for determining non-biased tests.

Second, once this analysis is complete and the criteria Judge Peckham set forth has been extracted, these criteria should be disseminated to a broad spectrum of "experts in the field." Not just "experts" who espouse the same views and opinions as the CDE. Remember the "experts" for the CDE were unable to help the department prevail in the Larry P. case (Larry P. v. Riles 1979). The "experts" to be used to evaluate criteria for selecting tests should include representatives of the Association of Black Psychologists (ABPsi). After all, ABPsi members were the "experts" for the plaintiffs who helped educate the court as to how standardized IQ tests were culturally biased.

Instead of following such a straightforward approach to seeking input concerning a procedure to effectively identify non-biased tests, the CDE has posed a lengthy list of questions which clearly indicated that the writer of those questions had ignored the most important, most publicized, most talked about legal decision affecting special education in our time. And similarly, the CDE question writers ignored the requirements in federal laws governing the use of IQ testing, as well as ignored the plethora of recent professional literature on the subject. The approach employed and the array of questions posed betrayed the motivation of the CDE.

Consequently, I feel compelled to respond to the questions in general terms and then to the unexpressed motivation of the CDE which is reflected in the questions. I am doing this in the hope that there are representatives from the CDE present and/or that members of the ITAP might be in the audience who will transmit these concerns to the superintendent of Public Instruction.

Time does not allow me the opportunity to respond to all of the thirty-seven questions, but I will address a few of the basic psychometric issues which are the focus of many of the questions, such as norming and standardization, item content and validity. First, the mandate of ITAP as I understand it is to identify a standardized intelligence test to replace those banned by the Larry P. court order (Larry P. v. Riles 1979). Those who understand the standardization process or the norming of a test will know that to replace one standardized test with another will only create the identical problem found by using the previous standardized test. The standardization process or the norming of a test discussed in detail in the Peckham decision is one source of cultural bias of a test (Green 1972). (I understand that Dr. Donald Ross Green, the author of that 1972 monograph "Racial and Ethnic Bias in Test Construction" is in the audience.)

Visualization of a bell curve or normal distribution will aid in understanding this process.

I assume we are all familiar with the properties of the normal curve. The range of scores will be distributed along the base so as to encompass 99 percent of the sample of scores. The scores clustered around the mean of the distribution make up the bell shape of the distribution of 68 percent of the scores. If the sample includes minorities of the same proportions as they exist in the population there should be approximately 10 percent African American in the distribution. If the scores of this group of African Americans clustered in one place in the distribution, they would not be large enough in number to offset the influence of the 68 percent majority group clustered around the mean or plus and minus one standard deviation. So it does not matter if there are African Americans or other minorities in the standardization sample; they will not have any influence on what is determined by the majority group in the sample to affect the "norm" for that distribution. Sophisticated sampling techniques will not overcome this reality. In other words, you cannot solve the problem of bias in a standardized test by replacing it with another standardized test.

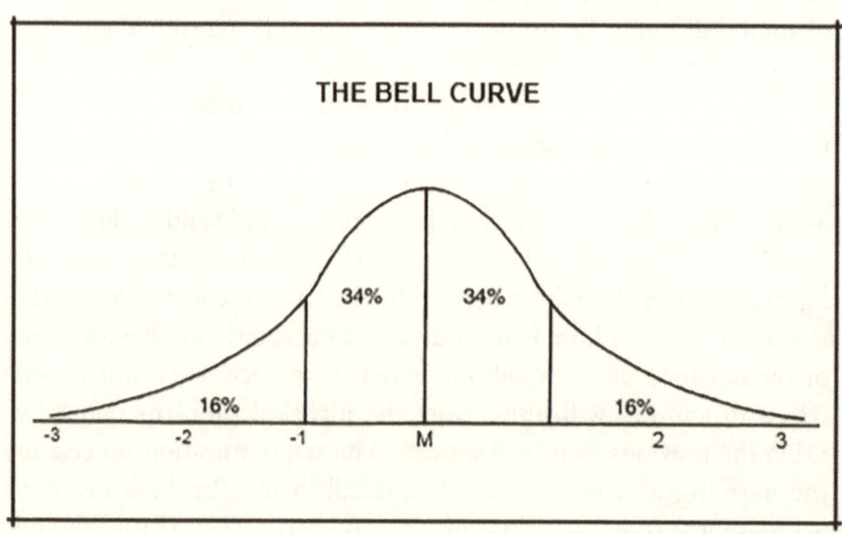

The case for item content bias is even more dramatic than the standardization phenomenon. If an individual has not had an opportunity to experience or gain knowledge of a situation, event, or circumstance and you question them about that situation, they are then at a disadvantage. When you ask the same question of an individual who has experienced that situation or event, they are more likely to be able to respond appropriately to the question. Examples of this type of cultural bias in test item content are numerous.

If you ask a child who has lived all of his/her life on an island such as Hawaii, "In what direction does the sun set?" You will mostly get the response, "Makai?" When you live on an island, the directional frame of reference is the sea or the mountains. In Hawaii, it is "Makai" or the mountains "Mouka." If you were to ask a child who lived all of his/her life in the inner city and had no opportunity to experience living in a rural setting, "If you were lost in the forest in the daytime, how would you find your way out of the forest?" That child would be at a disadvantage. These are but two of countless instances of item content bias that exist in standardized tests of intelligence.

The last area I will address of the concerns touched on in the ITAP questions is the issue of validity. Validity as a factor in test construction must be considered in context of the method used for determining validity. When a new test is developed, its validity is determined by how well the new test correlates with an existing test, which is presumed to be a valid measure of the trait or ability in question. So when a test maker produces a new IQ test, validity is determined by correlating the scores obtained on the new test with scores obtained, by the same subjects, on an established IQ test. If the old test is biased, a high correlation with the new test means that the new test is also biased. This is standard practice in the testing industry and began long before anyone seriously challenged the possible bias in standardized tests.

Another aspect of test validity relates to the fact that federal laws have been enacted which place strict requirements on the use of standardized tests with individuals with disabilities. Federal statutes stipulate that a test must be validated for the specific purpose for which it is used and that tests must be selected and administered in a fashion which is nondiscriminatory. There are no standardized tests of intelligence which have been validated for the specific purpose of placing African American children or any other ethnic group in special education. By applying the standardization and item content criteria, there are no tests on the market which can be said to be non-discriminatory. In other words, there are no commercially prepared standardized tests of intelligence which meet the federal requirements for assessment and placement of African American children in special education.

In an investigation of non-biased assessment procedures supported in part by the CDE, a committee of school psychologists, special educators, principals, and district administrators reviewed the Larry P. decision and a variety of assessment models described in the literature at the time and established the following criteria for the selection of alternative assessment models (Dent 1991).

Criterion number 1—Assessment models must meet federal legislative mandates requiring that instruments used be properly validated and nondiscriminatory.

Criterion number 2—Assessment models must be sensitive to the experiences of African American children, particularly to the linguistic cultural style of African Americans.

Criterion number 3—Assessment models must yield data which will identify specific problems in learning and will identify specific instructional remediations.

Criterion number 4—Assessment must not involve standardized, norm referenced tests.

My parting thought is that the California Department of Education, Special Education Commission, and the Intelligence Testing Advisory Panel give serious consideration to the above criteria for evaluating and selecting intelligence tests for use with African American students in California. My belief is that if they continue on the path they are currently taking as reflected in the questions presented in the communication I received from Dr. Thomas, we might well be back here thirty years hence exploring these very same issues. That is, you may be back here in thirty years. I don't think I have thirty more years to devote to this or any cause. So let's do everything we can to make sure they do it right this time.

Improving SAT Scores: Pros, Cons, Methods

William F. Brazziel (University of Connecticut, Storrs)

About seven thousand black high school seniors score 1,000 or above on the combined Scholastic Aptitude Tests (SAT). This places them at about the 80th percentile on these tests. The national average is about 900. About twenty-one thousand black high school seniors score 700 or below on the SAT (about the 15th percentile) and are a cause for concern in many circles. These proportions can be made more comparable, and this paper sets forth methods by which this can be achieved.

So much controversy surrounds the SAT that it is well to begin with a discussion of this dispute, including the pros and cons of making an effort to improve SAT scores in its context. A large number of individuals argue that it would be wise to use the time and effort necessary to raise SAT scores to concentrate on richer learning experiences which may or may not translate into higher SAT scores but which may serve black youths well as they grow into adulthood. Lynn Cheney, the director at the time of this writing of the National Endowment for the Humanities, for example, has stated flatly—on national television—that the SAT has little relationship to success in college and that students preparing for the SAT might better use their time to master the general curriculum more fully with an eye to doing well on achievement tests. The tests and their maker and progenitor, Educational Testing Service and the College Entrance Examination Board, have been investigated by a federal legislative body and sued by a truth-in-testing organization on the same grounds, i.e., lack of power of the SAT to predict success in college.

Many individuals are convinced that the tests are simply biased against minorities and women, and they can point out item after item to support this contention. As a result of charges of gender bias in scholarship awards based on the SAT, for example, the New York State Legislature in 1987 passed a law which directed administrators of the Empire and Regents scholarship programs to use grades as well as SAT scores to award these scholarships. Previously, SAT scores alone were used to select the winners, and over the years, boys had outnumbered girls—two is to one—among the scholarship winners. Girls score 61 points lower than boys on the SAT but have higher high school grade point averages. Empire and Regents scholarships are worth $10,000 each.

The test have also been the subject of a growing number of very incisive books. After reading David Owen's *None of the Above*, for example, one can no longer believe that all is well and nothing is wrong on the testing front. One can no longer believe that minority youths are treated fairly in either the testing or the highly unflattering press attending their performance. One can no longer ignore the advantages of rich over poor in the burgeoning coaching industry and in the virtual explosion of expensive computers and software designed to raise SAT scores of children of the well-to-do.

In response to criticism and as a result of their own experiences, some of America's best liberal arts colleges have dropped the SAT as an admissions requirement. Officials at Middlebury College in Vermont noted, for example, that SAT scores lacked predictive power. They noted that the best prediction the tests made was who could afford to go to coaching school. They went on to note that over 25 percent of their students had attended coaching schools and that this disturbed them greatly when they thought of the thousands of bright but poor youngsters who could not afford such schools. They were also disturbed by the lack of genuine educational value of coaching, quoting one student who noted that she did not have the time to spend nor the money to invest to turn herself into something that she was not.

Modifications of SAT requirements among colleges and universities may accelerate. In Rhode Island, Brown University students held a referendum on the test last spring and the margin of victory for the pro-SAT forces was only fifteen votes. A spokesman for the university noted that while they were observing the referendum carefully, the outcomes would not dictate policy.

In another development, Georgia has dropped SAT tests for students pursuing career programs in its community college system. They noted that the tests were of little value, that many of the students were intimidated by them, and that the state average on the SAT would rise if these students were excluded from the examinations. Some Georgia officials place great value on high state SAT averages, noting that they help the state industrial commission's efforts to attract industry.

A number of individuals have suggested that all colleges follow Georgia's lead and that the SAT be eliminated as a requirement for all community colleges and for all but the most selective colleges and universities. Such a policy would return the SAT to its origins. SAT testing began in 1941 with 10,000 students being tested as a service for 45 selective colleges and universities. Since then, some 1500 colleges have responded to invitations to become members of the College Entrance Examination Board. A condition of membership is SAT testing of entrants to the college. Observers have noted that on 70 percent of the campuses of member colleges, the tests are given almost no weight at all in admissions decisions. As a condition of membership, however, the policy of requiring the tests remains in force.

Finally, in this vein, a growing number of colleges now accept other tests in lieu of the SAT, e.g., Armed Forces Qualifications Tests (AFQT), General Education Development Tests (GED), Civil Service Tests, and the like. Many are good predictors of college success. The day may come when ETS will offer students a choice of tests at their testing sessions: SAT, GED, AFQT, et al. Students' choices would depend upon the tests accepted for admission by the colleges to which they will apply.

In light of criticisms discussed above, it is understandable that a decision to mount an intensive effort to raise SAT scores of black students would give one pause. A number of individuals would regard the effort as a surrender in a fight against a biased instrument. Others would point out the lack of predictive power of the test and the hardships placed on youths from families with modest means in trying to prepare for and take a test with seemingly little value. Still others would decry the placement of these youths in what is often termed no-win situations where they must compete with affluent youths who are routinely sent to coaching schools and availed of the new computers and SAT software for self-coaching.

In the face of this criticism, a goal, other than (or in addition to) parity in SAT scores for black youth, must be set forth if an effort is to be mounted. A starting point, perhaps, is the recognition that SAT scores of black students are already increasing and that any effort to be mounted would be an effort to accelerate an ongoing process. Black SAT means have increased fifty points over the past decade with little direct effort on anyone's part, it seems. The rate of increase is miniscule, however (about five points per year), and at the present rate of increase three decades will be required before black students reach the national average on the test. Acceleration in this context is surely desirable.

A second point to note in this respect is that the SAT is really an achievement test and, like other achievement tests, it is an indicator, of sorts, of the outcomes of schooling. The College Board now uses the term "developed abilities" instead of aptitude when discussing what tests measure. Donald Stewart, the new president of the College Board, has pointed out in his first public statements that students do better on the SAT when they take a full schedule of college preparatory courses in high school. He noted that this was especially true for black students. Stewart is the former president of Spelman College, an old line historically black institution. Hopefully, the College Board will soon change the name of the tests from Scholastic Aptitude Tests to Developed Abilities Tests (DAT instead of SAT) to match its new rhetoric and its retreat from earlier contention that the tests measured some mysterious innate forces which were immune to instruction.

In the end, the new view of the SAT as an achievement test which is profoundly affected by type and quality of schooling, coupled with the visibility of the SAT, is the most compelling reason to move ahead with an accelerated effort to improve SAT scores of black youths. The importance of this reason cannot be overestimated. People accept the criticisms of Owen and truth-in-testing organizations, for example, but cling to the SAT because of its visibility as a measure of the quality of the schooling. As such, the SAT will continue to be the "only game in town" until new procedures emerge for admitting students to college and, of equal importance, maintaining the pecking order of high schools and colleges. This may happen one day, but it will be a gradual process at best. Parents pay huge sums of money to assure high SAT scores for their children and get them into colleges where the various rating guides—and cocktail party chitchat—indicate that the SAT average is high.

Important here is that black parents and others can insist that SAT scores of their children be improved and do whatever is necessary to bring this about. The goal of improved SAT scores is completely recognizable by all concerned, i.e., school board members, teachers, students, and parents and the fruits of their efforts are there for all to see in annual reports of SAT means for the young people. Vague insistence on quality education or better education will bring vague reports of improvement. Insistence on SAT score improvement will bring specific and highly visible reports of improvement.

Success in raising SAT scores of black youths will result in higher scores for black youths on other tests. This is also a compelling reason to move ahead with efforts to improve SAT scores of black youths. More black youths, for example, will score high enough to qualify for apprenticeship programs, the armed forces, favored schools with the armed forces, civil service jobs, corporate entry level jobs, and training programs within the corporations. The new view of the SAT as an achievement test dictates such. Achievement tests correlate highly with each other. Indeed, over half of the achievement tests on the market list correlation with other achievement tests as the only method of satisfying requirements for predictive validity. So adequate SAT scores translate into adequate AFQT scores, adequate civil service test scores, and on and on. A need exists here. The New York Telephone Company, for example, recently reported that 84 percent of the applicants failed its latest test for entry-level jobs. Vocabulary skills, number relationships, and problem-solving skills, all similar—or identical in some cases—to the contents of the SAT were the principal components of the test. If intensified efforts to accelerate improvement of SAT scores among black students are mounted, what form could these efforts take? What methods to generate increases could be employed? Curriculum and coaching are two tried and true methods of raising SAT scores and any broad effort to accelerate improvement of SAT scores among black youth would utilize both methods. These methods are discussed below along with the difficulties involved in availing black children and youth of each.

Curriculum

As Stewart and others have noted, placing larger numbers of black youths in college preparatory curricula will result in higher SAT scores for black seniors. This is a basic thrust in efforts to raise SAT scores. There is a serious gap between what youths learn in general and college preparatory curricula and a significant difference between the numbers of black and white youth pursuing these curricula. These differences have gone unnoticed, and, like high blood pressure, they could be regarded as a silent academic killer. Indeed the gap is so unnoticed that the US Department of Education had to make a special computer run to generate data on the black/white gap in college prep enrollments when such was requested by this writer. Data were finally generated from the department's longitudinal study of the attributes and afterschool experiences of a national random sample of students who graduated from high school in 1982. The study is entitled "High School and Beyond," and the data showed that only 36 percent of the black high school graduates were enrolled in college preparatory curricula, about a third fewer than those who took the SAT and ACT tests for that year. Many low scores, it seems, stem from black youths enrolled in general or vocational courses of study who took the SAT or ACT anyway and, presumably, went on to college. Nearly half of the white graduates, on the other hand (47 percent), were enrolled in college preparatory courses.

One has only to read a few pages of Jeannie Oakes' book, *Keeping Track*, to understand—and become alarmed—about the general/college preparatory gap between black and white students. To research her book, Oakes attended a large number of general and college preparatory classes to compare learning experiences of the two. In English classes in the general track, Oakes found that students spent much of their time (1) completing workbook exercises and drills; (2) practicing the completion of job applications; (3) discussing current events, the rock scene, and similar topics; and (4) reading youth life and adventure books. Students in college preparatory English classes spent much of their time (1) reading Shakespeare, Keats, and Browning; (2) writing weekly theme papers and receiving feedback; (3) using computers tor SAT preparation drill; and (4) studying reports and papers from college freshman English.

One would surmise that students exposed to such strikingly different curricula tor four years would have strikingly different SAT scores at the end of the period. This is indeed true. A request to the College Entrance Examination Board tor data on SAT scores according to curriculum brought a report which showed that black students enrolled in college preparatory curricula scored 124 points higher on the combined SAT than black students enrolled in general curricula. The gap tor those in vocational curricula was worse. As noted above, these students have to take the SAT as a requirement tor entry to career programs in community colleges. SAT gaps of black students become much more understandable when all of this is considered. Large numbers of black students are enrolled in career programs in community colleges.

While pursuit of college preparatory curricula by greater numbers of black students must be basic in any effort to raise SAT scores of black students, such a pursuit will not be easy to engender. Many black students are tracked away from college prep curricula. This tracking begins on the first day of school and involves entrance and readiness tests. An observer of a New York school system patiently explained the process to the writer. It goes as follows: The Metropolitan Readiness Test is administered at the end of kindergarten. The scores from this test are sent to the elementary schools the children attend. Children who score high on these tests are placed in fast classrooms. The others are placed in slow classrooms. Good teachers are placed in the fast classrooms. Bad teachers are placed in the slow classrooms. A fast pace—more homework, more discussion, more pages covered—is found in the fast classrooms. A slow pace is found in the slow classrooms. Children in the fast classrooms are welcome additions to the student body. Children in the slow classrooms are tolerated. Children can move from slow classrooms to fast classrooms if they work hard at the end of each school year, according to stated policy. Few do, it seems. According to the observer, the children in slow classrooms keep getting slower, and the children in the fast classrooms keep getting faster. The differences in the paces and the demands of the classrooms see to this. And it all starts with a kindergarten test.

What a sad story. A wise person once said that one could receive a good education without scoring well on tests but would probably not be allowed to do so. The situation for many black students illustrates this in graphic terms. Tests reign supreme. If the strategy of accelerating black student scores through increased enrollments of black students in college preparatory curricula is to be pursued, the problems of tracking described above must be addressed. What can be done? School boards can be apprised of the shortfalls in college preparatory enrollment among black students. Lawsuits can be filed against boards that do not take action to ameliorate the situation. Enrollment of black students in college preparatory curricula can become an issue in school board elections and appointments—and in politics generally.

School boards can be forced to come to grips with policies that result in shortfalls in black enrollment in college preparatory curricula, but there are also sociopsychological barriers to overcome. This author helped a mostly black group stage a mighty battle in one community recently over barriers to enrollment in college preparatory courses in the high schools. The school board finally agreed that anybody could take anything in the high schools. This was a victory for democracy and the American way, but to our dismay, an appreciable increase of black students enrolling in college preparatory courses was not forthcoming. School mores dictated that black students should enter general and vocational programs, for the most part, and the students continued to do this. If the strategy of higher SAT scores through higher enrollment in college is to be pursued, we need elementary and junior high schools which prepare more black children psychologically to enroll in college preparatory curricula.

The most important thing we can do in psychological preparation for college prep enrollment is to have larger numbers of black children come out of the elementary schools with strong academic skills and with considerable test acumen. Elementary school teachers and principals, of course, are quick to point out that parents and communities must send more children to the school who are academically competent, and they will strongly emphasize that the development of academic competence begins at birth. They are surely right in many cases. More intensive academic preparation is needed for many children at an earlier age. The antidotes to this problem are both short-range and long-range in nature. The short-range antidote is a redoubling of efforts to prepare the children regardless of deficits they may have. Two recent national conferences on the education of black children brought together many principals, superintendents, and teachers from schools where the ideas of the late Ronald Edmonds are being utilized to good advantage. Edmonds was a diligent worker in the More Effective Schools movement. Black children in these schools score at the national level on tests and large numbers of them will be placed in college preparatory curricula in the high schools. These remarkable conferences were sponsored by a coalition of educators, civil rights groups, and legislators.

Enrollment of larger numbers of black children in earlier early education, e.g., cradle schools, infant schools, and day care centers that teach, is the long-range antidote. This strategy will help children who otherwise would bring serious academic deficits to the schools. Reading well, developing IQ abstract-thinking patterns, and scoring well on tests are all strongly related to language development and the development of thinking habits at an early age. Academic skills and test acumen among children can be developed at a later age, but it is a more difficult proposition. This is especially true for the rather large numbers of black children born to undereducated mothers and cared for most of their waking hours by undereducated grandmothers. The strongest correlation with test acumen is attention and informal teaching at an early age by educated adults. Sandra Scarr and Richard Weinberg, for example, found that IQ and other test scores for black children adopted by white middle-class parents matched national norms. Further, they found that the earlier the adoption, the higher the scores. Jane Mercer found similar test acumen in studies of children in black middle-class families.

One obvious answer to the problem of rich educational experiences at an early age, of course, is to have more black children raised by black (or white) middle-class families. A huge problem here, however, is the small number of children among black middle-class families. In listings of numbers of children among various types of American families, black middle-class families perennially bring up the rear with 1.2 children per family. Since 2.11 children are required for replacement of a given population or group, the black middle class will not become a self-perpetuating entity until black middle-class couples adopt more children. This is to say that this group will not be able to replace itself but must depend upon upward mobility from the classes below it to maintain its numbers. Expansion of the numbers of second and third generation black middle-class parents under these circumstances is slow at best. White middle-class families have low birth rates also, but their birth rates are closer to the replacement threshold than rates of the black middle class.

Said differently, population replacement among the white middle-class comes from middle-class families to a great extent and many white children are thus assured of the early and enriched educational experiences that middle-class families afford their children. Black middle-class replacement does not come from middle-class families to a great extent but from upwardly mobile working-class families. Thus, fewer black children are given the early and enriched educational experiences afforded by middle-class families. This is a profound demographic fact, and it affects SAT scores as surely as anything else we might discuss. It relates to SAT performance in this way: early, enriched educational experiences in middle-class homes result in apt kindergarten children who score well on readiness tests. High-scoring kindergarten children enter fast elementary school classes and score well on achievement tests. High-scoring elementary children enter fast junior high school classes. High-scoring junior high school students enter college preparatory curricula in high schools. College preparatory students score well on SAT tests. Planners ignore the demographics/SAT connection at the peril of a failed long-range strategy for improving SAT performance of large numbers of black youth.

If black middle-class families continue to have small families, what can be done to improve school readiness and test acumen of children from other classes to enable them to become apt kindergartners, gain access to fast classes in the elementary schools, gain access to college preparatory schools in the high schools, and make adequate SAT scores? We must employ earlier early education programs to do the job. School and community programs already exist to help pupils and students at risk, and they can be expanded to take very young children. Head start is such a case, and there are a number of infant and toddler schools in operation although most are underfunded. A recent report of the Committee for Economic Development called for very large investments in earlier early education for children at risk, e.g., cradle schools, toddler schools, and more. This committee is comprised of corporate heads and influential educators, and we may see an expansion of such programs soon.

It is important that school programs constantly maintain the gains of early education for children at risk and constantly seek to strengthen academic skills for their young charges. Most importantly, a concern for test acumen must be high on the agenda of faculty and administrators in the schools these children attend. Early education and more effective schools can send an ever larger stream of academically-strong, test-wise children into the high schools. Sadly, in too many cases, a concern for test acumen is not a priority for some of the teachers, principals, coordinators, supervisors, and superintendents who staff the schools. A discussion group at a recent national conference of educators in such schools, for example, did not view development of test acumen among their young charges with very much enthusiasm. A Los Angeles principal noted that she had broached the subject to her faculty and was told that the children did not have the ability to develop test acumen. Several teachers contended that what the children needed was warmth, love, and encouragement, and their academic skills would naturally follow. Others advanced the notion that a better understanding of their roots would help the children. The discussion was discouraging to say the least. We must do whatever is necessary to modify these views. Test acumen must be taught as a matter of course and this instruction must begin early. It is encouraging to note that discussion groups elsewhere at the conference heard report after report from school principals and teachers who took great pride in the fact that every grade in their school was "on level." That means that the average achievement test score for every grade in the school matched or exceeded the national level. Conferees gave a standing ovation at the announcement of the achievement of the Atlanta school system where all grades in all schools are now "on level." The schools in Atlanta are 87 percent black.

Coaching

As noted above, white high school juniors and seniors regularly go to Stanley Kaplan, Princeton Review, and similar coaching schools to improve their SAT scores. About ten years ago, the National Association of Secondary School Principals joined the club and commissioned the development of an elegant computer software package designed to boost SAT scores. The initial price for the package was $795. Many schools in affluent neighborhoods bought twenty to twenty-five software packages and twenty to twenty-five computers on which to run them. The computers cost $3000 each at the time. PTAs pitched in to help where is necessary. Many parents installed computers and SAT packages in their homes and toddlers were urged to begin their SAT preparation on these machines.

Black students do not participate in very much of this type of preparation and shortfalls in coaching, like shortfalls in college prep enrollments, take their toll on black SAT scores. The exact numbers of white juniors and seniors who attend coaching schools is not known—neither high school nor college officials like to discuss this. A third or more of white juniors and seniors may be a good estimate when discussing numbers of students attending these schools. Whatever until coaching is eliminated—and it may never be—black juniors and seniors must have a higher rate of participation in coaching. Many cannot afford such rates, of course. Commercial coaching firms note in press releases designed to deflect criticism of their operations that they offer scholarships to needy students but few if any of these benefactions have been in evidence. An excellent addition to federal programs designed to improve chances of college success for needy students could be vouchers to attend coaching schools or funds for Upward Bound programs to add coaching classes to their offerings.

Communities can be mobilized to help in coaching. Marian Wright Edelman noted in a recent address that a visit to Japan convinced her that black American churches and community groups could very well adopt the widespread system of educational *jukus* which Japanese communities use to good advantage. *Jukus* are tutoring centers and after-school classes run by community groups to help children keep pace and to help youths prepare for college entrance examinations. A good starting point in black American *jukus* might well be investments by churches, community centers, lodges, sororities, fraternities, and social clubs in computers and SAT software and in the operation of SAT software classes.

Someday, colleges and universities will identify students who have been coached and review their SAT scores with this fact in mind. Someday, funds will be offered to researchers interested in determining the integrity of SAT scores which have been raised by coaching. When that day comes, coaching mania will subside. Until that day comes, black students will have to participate more fully in coaching.

Curriculum and coaching

An approach to improving the SAT scores of black youths which combines curriculum and coaching can be very effective and can lessen dependence on schools to do the job alone. Many schools are simply incapable of mounting efforts like this. American education is very uneven in quality. Some sixteen thousand school districts are involved in education along with 3.1 million teachers, aides, and administrators. Even the definition of quality is vague at best. Preparatory school curricula are effective vehicles for raising SAT scores and strengthening academic skills, and they are used to good advantage by many people. Some of the more striking successes have been achieved by the preparatory schools of the armed services. The US Air Force Academy, for example, has built a beautiful facility, the US Air Force Preparatory School, on its campus. The US Navy sends students to its prep school at Newport, Rhode Island, and the US Army to its school at Fort Dix, New Jersey. Hundreds of private prep schools take high school graduates for a year of enrichment. Invariably, high SAT scores result from the prep school experience.

Prep schools are expensive and many students do not need a full year to fill a few gaps in their preparation and to develop SAT test acumen. Good summer schools can do the trick if they concentrate on these tasks and if students are devoted to them.

The Minnesota Institute of Technology of the University of Minnesota operates one of the better curriculum/coaching summer schools. Using a foundation grant, the institute hired Stanley Kaplan, president of Stanley Kaplan Inc., to serve as a continuing consultant to help faculty members design and deliver a curriculum that would strengthen certain academic areas of minority students headed for prestigious engineering schools and which would, at the same time, improve SAT performance. Minority juniors and seniors attend the school with full scholarships. They also receive a stipend of $600 to make up for lost wages from summer jobs. The school runs for the better part of the summer and is quite successful. The curriculum is SAT math, SAT English, and SAT test skills. Students attend six hours a day and work hard. They come away with SAT scores which enable them to gain admission to some of the most prestigious engineering schools in America. With three hundred or so colleges and universities receiving foundation and federal funds to develop curriculum/coaching schools, black performance on SAT tests could be immensely improved.

Corporations may also be tapped for support for this sort of program. A careful reading of the business section of the July 12, 1987 issue of the *New York Times* reveals how deeply involved corporations have become in precollege education for minority youths. Self-interest is the driving force here. Demographers tell us that over a third of the work force in 1999 will be comprised of members of minority groups. The new cry from corporate board rooms is "train every brain." Colleges and universities looking for support for programs like the one at Minnesota may find willing benefactors among corporations in their states and regions. Curriculum/coaching schools would seem a natural for black colleges and universities, many of which operated campus academies and prep schools long after schools like Harvard and Princeton phased out theirs. Wilberforce Academy, with many living alumni, is such a case.

Conclusions

More black youths can make high SAT scores. Concentration on SAT score improvement will develop academic skills and test acumen which will enable black students to do well on other tests. As a result, more black youths will qualify for job entry and for in-house training programs. They will also qualify in greater numbers for the military services for favored training programs in the services, for apprenticeship programs, government jobs, and more.

The SAT and the coaching industry which has grown up around it are both controversial. Until America decides to use other college admission measures more widely; however, black youths must be availed of the college preparatory programs and the curriculum and coaching which will raise other test scores.

Effective means of raising SAT scores already exist. Money and people to make the effort succeed are needed.

See appendix, tables 1 and 2 for additional alternatives to the SAT.

Implications of IQ Testing for Mental Health Treatment of African Americans

William B. Lawson

African American health care: some general considerations

Sometimes, there is a cognitive disconnect between research findings and their use in professional practice. In the 1950s, there was a good deal of research which showed the negative impact of segregated schools in Virginia; at the same time, there were other studies that showed a higher incidence of mental illness among African Americans in integrated schools. Policy makers used the latter findings to justify decisions not to integrate the schools.

Is there a conspiracy, some plot, some underlying assumption, or a basic misunderstanding about the potential usefulness of advances in research technology? A cursory look at epidemiological research of the 1970s shows that more African Americans died more quickly than everyone else. If African Americans had died at the same rate as everyone else, we would have had between sixty thousand to one hundred thousand more African Americans alive each year. One argument for the discrepancy is that African Americans have an impaired immune system and are destined to become ill and die more quickly than everyone else.

Evidence is abundant that we are a hardy race, but we are less likely to get medical treatment that is commonly provided for others. There is evidence, for example, that African Americans are more likely to contract hypertension than the population at large which may be related to the foods we eat. Since the incidence of hypertension increases the risk of strokes and morbidity that comes from that risk, we should develop better ways to identify hypertension. If we could get African Americans into the health care system sooner, if preventive treatment could be provided, the likelihood of strokes would be reduced along with medical and social costs. Rather than look at people as being expendable, we need to develop ways to provide better access to better treatment.

When the argument was made that perhaps treatment was not as effective in the African American community as it was in the white community, the response in some quarters was that African Americans were intellectually inferior and thus were not readily able to comply with treatment. Quite to the contrary, there is overwhelming evidence that many African Americans just do not have access to physicians due to low income.

Africans on the continent do not have the rates of hypertension that our people have in the United States. This fact destroys the hypothesis that we are genetically prone to contract this disease. Something happened between the time when we were there and when we came here that has increased our risk for hypertension. Something else happened that resulted in our babies having lower birth weight than those on the African continent. In African countries, despite higher rates of poverty, undeveloped technology, and a less sophisticated health care system, African babies are bigger than our babies.

African-Americans and the mental health system

A recent headline in one tabloid magazine exclaimed, "Psychiatry and the betrayal of African American mental health." My first thought was, "Oh my god, what now? Someone is making a scandal at our expense." Historically, however, our treatment in the mental health system in this country has been nothing if not scandalous. Among the more glaring examples is the following: During slavery, African Americans were diagnosed with mental disorders based on the fact that they ran away from their masters. They were prescribed several kinds of medicines for these "mental disorders" with the hope of preventing runaways. One such disorder, Ephesia Ethiopia, was thought to be pathological and resulted in many referrals to the equivalent of a psychologist.

How much has changed since slavery? If you look at mental health care in this country, many African Americans perceive it to be more pathological to them than helpful. Reasons include problems of misdiagnosis and excessive reliance on psychotropic and antidepressant medicines. For example, African Americans are much more likely to be misdiagnosed with schizophrenia when they have nothing wrong or have other disorders such as anxiety and depression. Attention deficit disorders are diagnosed in African American children ten to twenty times more frequently than they are in white children. Some psychiatrists doubt that such a disorder exists. While I believe it exists, I certainly do not believe it occurs ten to twenty times more frequently in our children than it does in white children. In African Americans, the disorder has a tendency to "disappear" in later life and become exclusively a disorder of white folks.

The evidence is pretty clear that African Americans receive substandard care in our mental health system. We are much more likely to be involuntarily committed, given medicine rather than psychotherapy, and to be terminated early from treatment rather than to receive long-term rehabilitation services. Many of the psychiatric disorders that we encounter today are considered to be primarily brain diseases. In some ways that is good because it removes blame from the family. However, when we attribute schizophrenia or attention deficit disorder to biological causes, treatment is beyond the scope of training for most mental health providers. Quality mental health services, in this instance, are made further beyond the reach of most African Americans. By implication, IQ tests are not needed; instead, we need to develop novel alternative ways to deliver mental health services to an underserved population.

Historically speaking, there has been a determined effort by psychiatry to find pathology in African Americans that will explain their lowered 10 scores. Could it be that once it is determined that we cannot benefit from treatment, there is no need to provide services? This was the hypothesis suggested by Murray's *The Bell Curve*. On its face, this is a very simplistic hypothesis because, thanks to Asa Hilliard, we can now see clearly several cracks in *The Bell Curve*. Whether intelligence is influenced more by heredity or by the environment is a question yet to be answered. We do know that through environmental manipulations, a person's IQ score can vary.

We might expect that the IQ score of Muhammad Ali would be lower than it was previously due to the fact that he has developed Parkinson's-like symptoms. (He was tested several times by the military.) He has a disorder that is affecting his ability to express his intelligence; his intelligence has not been affected by his disorder. Most importantly, if you were to give an IQ test to Muhammad Ali and conclude that he is a vegetable, which the military attempted to do, you would be run out of town. There can be no doubt that this man is highly intelligent.

A CAT scan is one technique that is used to study the living human brain. We can determine its functioning by looking at activity in different parts. When looking at a cross section of a normal human brain (slide please), there is a nice outline of the brain with the yellow areas representing activity. In contrast (slide please), this is the brain of a heavy cocaine and alcohol abuser. We know that cocaine and alcohol, even after a person stops using them, can produce long-term impairment (as much as 90 percent reduction) in cognitive functioning that can be measured by testing with the Wechsler intelligence test and other measures. Thus, we know that environmental factors can lower the measured IQ of many folks. What happens to someone with a head injury that results in intellectual decline? If they were formerly high functioning, do we tell them they are no longer useful? Medical science has many resources to help these folks get back to their previous level of functioning.

Based on data that my colleagues and I collected in a community in Little Rock, Arkansas, which had one of the highest murder rates in the country, we found many children who were not doing well in school. We found that many of these children had experienced traumatic events throughout much of their young lives. Several of them told us that they had seen people arrested and beaten by the police; they were used to seeing people being shot, and seeing dead bodies were common experiences which they had. Our findings were in accord with research in a Detroit public school where 20 percent of children had seen someone shot. Several of the children were diagnosed with attention deficit disorders. Many had been given IQ tests on which they performed poorly. They were often placed in special education because regular education did not have resources to deal with them.

According to *The Bell Curve*, such children are genetically inferior. However, through summer enrichment programs, a number of the children in our study went from failing grades to average or above. We did not conduct formal IQ testing, but Dr. Asa Hilliard has reported increases in IQ scores by as much as 20 points in similar programs. These children were suffering from a phenomenon called post-traumatic stress disorder in which folks exposed to catastrophic events such as war or other environmental hazards will show a variety of emotional and cognitive deficits that are reversible if appropriate interventions are made in a timely manner. Where does this lead us in terms of the IQ question? Is there a problem?

There is much evidence that IQ tests are used in just the opposite way they were intended to be used. Rather than using them for diagnosis, treatment, or for identifying how folks can be successful, they are all too often used to exclude folks who may have great potential for being successful.

The Status of Special Education in the Los Angeles Unified School District

Sandra Cox

Let me begin by saying, thank God for affirmative action. I would not be here today had it not been available when I went to graduate school. I was teaching for the Los Angeles Unified School District in 1965, the year I started graduate school. As a result of the

Watts uprising, our school district felt the need to hire more African American school psychologists. The district in collaboration with the federal government's Model Cities Program established a grant that made available money to pursue a degree in psychology for African American teachers who lived in South Central, Los Angeles. Thus, I applied and was accepted to study psychology at California State University at Los Angeles.

You have heard much about the history of testing African Americans from Dr. Robert Williams this morning and will no doubt hear more this afternoon from Dr. Harold Dent, both of whom are my mentors. For this reason, I will omit most of the discussion I had planned in this area. We heard Dr. Williams speak of the malevolent philosophy that European psychologists such as Goddard, Yerkes, Terman, Brigam, and others had for developing intelligence tests at the turn of the century—which was primarily to exclude people of color from participating in the American dream. That same philosophy appears not to have changed much despite the civil rights movement and Larry P. If we listen to views of contemporary European psychologists such as Shockley, Jensen, Herrenstein, Lambert, Sattler, Murray (the list goes on), we know that racism in testing is alive and well.

This brings to mind a tale of the emperor who had no clothes. Let IQ tests represent the emperor, we then see that contemporary European psychologists, recognizing that the emperor had been defrocked by black psychologists, provided him with a new regal outfit plus battle gear. But black psychologists such as Asa Hilliard, Robert Williams, and Harold Dent discovered that even the emperor's new clothes were cheap and transparent. In other words, the emperor is still nude. Lacking in validity, IQ tests cannot measure human potential no matter how much you dress them up. They are neither non-biased, nondiscriminatory, nor culture-free.

In our school district (LAUSD) during the year 1997, the number of African Americans in classes for the EMR was 856; this was 270 more students in EMR classes than there should have been, based on their percentage in the student population. If we look at the numbers of African Americans in classes for the seriously emotionally disturbed (SED), we would see a similar problem. African American students comprised 513 when there should only have been 151, again based on their percentage in the student population. Despite the ban on testing African Americans for special education in California, such testing continues to play a significant role in the disproportionate number of African Americans being placed in special education classes in Los Angeles.

One promising development for rectifying the situation in the Los Angeles Unified School District took place when a recent lawsuit was filed. In November 1993, the American Civil Liberties Union Foundation of Southern California and the law firm of Newman, Aarans, and Vanaman filed a class action lawsuit on behalf of district students with disabilities alleging that the district had failed to comply with its special education obligations under the Federal Individuals with Disabilities Act. More specifically, the plaintiffs alleged that the district had pervasively and continuously failed to search for and identify students with disabilities in order to provide for their education in a timely manner. The district denied the allegations but invited plaintiffs to explore the possibility of narrowing the issues, if not actually settling the case. The parties agreed to a multistep approach to resolving the dispute. First, the plaintiffs submitted a list of specific instances where they contended the district was violating the special education laws, together with a list of recommended policy and practice changes. The district responded by agreeing to the relief sought by the plaintiffs, that is, to provide services that were required by law

There were, however, areas where counsel for both sides disagreed on the scope of the problem, the requirements of the law, and the remedial measures required. Instead of suffering the expense of discovery and risk of trial, the parties agreed to retain expert consultants to investigate the issues, make findings concerning the district's compliance with special education laws and make nonbinding recommendations for the district to meaningfully improve service. Both parties agreed to review the findings and recommendations, adopt a final settlement, and otherwise resolve the litigation.

Total Personnel Assessment: A Case Study in Affirmative Action— City of Santa Ana, California

Joseph Canton

This topic, "Total Personnel Assessment: A Case Study in Affirmative Action—City of Santa Ana, California" is the title of my dissertation (Canton 1976). It is focused on a process that was designed to increase the number of African American police officers in a small city.

The Civil Rights Commission, established in 1969, reported that the unemployment rate was far greater for African Americans than the white majority in every major geographic area of the United States, that they were even underrepresented in state and local governments. The picture looked especially dismal when the nation suffered economic decline.

Beginning in 1976, governmental agencies were required to develop job-related tests that could be validated in an effort to achieve affirmative action goals. Using the case study method, I examined the city of Santa Ana's effort to develop a process that was allegedly free of bias so that more minority policemen could be hired. The first step in the process involved the hiring of an outside consultant to perform a job analysis to determine what tasks were necessary to perform the work of a police officer. Nine factors were identified: (1) human relations, (2) learning ability, (3) motivation, (4) written communication, (5) ability to work under stress, (6) personal conduct, (7) physical condition, (8) common sense judgment, and (9) oral communication. Performance on these variables was the main criteria for which a candidate was selected to be a police officer in the city of Santa Ana, California. I learned that African Americans scored consistently highest on factor 8, common sense judgment which was defined as the ability to obtain proper information and directions from fellow officers and supervisors; the ability to size up the element of danger when making an arrest, knows when to retreat or attack, knows when to use force, knows how to use proper procedures when handling accidents, family disputes, fights, robberies, and other emergencies. African Americans also did well on factor 9, oral communication.

"Total Personnel Assessment" was described as a "holistic" approach to screening candidates. In other words, doing poorly on any single factor was not a cause for elimination. All candidates were examined on all factors including a confidential psychological test. This pilot study consisted of 452 candidates who were given a one-hour interview. The entire process cost the city $2.5 million.

Findings and conclusion

After the smoke had cleared, African Americans were selected at a rate much lower than other candidates despite having completed more years of education—some had bachelor degrees. *How could this be*, I wondered, *if the process was "scientific" and "free of bias"?*

Even though African Americans did well on job-related tasks, most candidates were still eliminated. A case cannot be made for or against the IQ test since it was factored into the total assessment process. Despite Santa Ana's effort, the rate of hiring African Americans for its police force has not changed appreciably over the years since the pilot project. For example, there were seven African Americans on Santa Ana's police force in 1976 and six in 1998. It is my conclusion that without quotas, there will be no change in the employment rate of African Americans.

CHAPTER 6

African American Consumer's Bill of Legal Testing Rights on Standardized Testing

Vernon G. Gettone, John Affeldt, and Harold E. Dent

Most African American people know very little of how standardized tests affect their lives. Standardized IQ, aptitude and achievement tests determine what schools we attend, what kind of education we receive, and what kind of jobs we are hired to do during our careers. They are gatekeepers to our children and to us as consumers. Before we agree to take a standardized test or give permission to our children to be tested, we should know certain things about tests. We have a right to know!

Before you decide to agree to have your child tested, ask the test givers to answer some basic questions. Do not consent to participate until these are answered to your satisfaction in plain English. If they cannot be answered in plain English, the person who is explaining is probably not competent to give the test or the test is dangerous (unfair, not valid, culturally biased) or no good.

Basic questions for test givers

- What are standardized tests?
- Why are you planning to give this test to my child?
- Are the tests being used given in the language that my child understands best?
- Will the tests used compare my child to other children from the same cultural background? Or will the other cultural background be different?
- What educational need does the test identify?
- What special school program or practice will be employed to remedy the need identified?
- Will the information gained on this test or the procedure used hurt my child or me in any way?
- Can this test alone determine my child's placement in the classroom?
- Will you put what you said about the test and my child in writing?
- Have any studies been done on large numbers of African American students to support that the test is valid for them?

Bill of rights to standardized testing

- You have a right to know what any test is measuring in your child and what the dangers are of using it.
- You have a right to know if African Americans have scored well on this test and have benefited from the results.
- You have a right to know if the test was developed with the experience of African American people (language, vocabulary, values, and examples of everyday life) in mind.
- You have a right to know how qualified the people are who give, interpret, or use the test, what direct experiences they have had with African American people, and how much knowledge they have of African American culture.

- You have a right to know what test scores or test reports are kept in personal records (Freedom of Information Act 1996).
- You have a right to know who has access to the information in personal records. You also have a right to examine your child's academic records. If these records contain test scores, you have a right to see those scores as well (Family Education Rights and Privacy Act of 1974, also known as the Buckley Amendment).
- You have a right for your child to have due process. For example, your child must get adequate notice when a test is required for high school graduation and adequate time to prepare for the test.
- You have a right to expect the schools to provide your child fair and equitable treatment. Schools cannot, for example, have different test score requirements based on gender or race.
- You have a right to request and receive postponement of your child's evaluation until it can be done appropriately by a qualified test giver.
- You have a right to be tested by, or have the test results interpreted by a qualified person of your choice, and in whom you have confidence.
- You have a right to refuse to be tested, and you have a right to refuse to give consent to allow your child to be tested.

This document was originally prepared as the "Black Consumer's Bill of Rights and Guide to Standardized Testing" for the Association of Black Psychologists by Asa G. Hilliard III, EdD, and Harold E. Dent, PhD, in January 1977.

EPILOGUE

Participants at the symposium on IQ testing of African Americans could have been forgiven for thinking they had traveled back thirty years in time. Battles that black psychologists had successfully litigated and debated in the literature appear not to have really been won. Black children are still being tracked into dead-end psychological traps that condemn them to a life of misery. However, the march of progress infused the event as we heard about the possibilities of the Learning Potential Assessment Device, enrichment programs, and additional litigation to make accurate readings of the true state of young minds in a diverse population.

Since the time of Carter G. Woodson, we've known the strategies to create effective learning environments for African American students. Nothing in the intervening time has provided any solid evidence that the psychometric movement embodied by IQ testing has any value for African American children. The topic papers presented in this volume illuminate the many cultural and socioeconomic issues that the testing movement infuses into its instruments. The mandate for the new millennium is the same one that bubbled up in the 1960s—end the testing of black children with instruments calculated to perpetuate their subjugation and replace those instruments with real diagnostic tools that mine their inherent potential.

BIOGRAPHICAL SKETCHES

John T. Affeldt, Esq., received his bachelor of arts degree in English from Stanford University at Stanford, California, and his law degree from Harvard Law School at Cambridge, Massachusetts. As managing attorney for Public Advocates at San Francisco, California, he is the lead counsel in AMAE v. California, a precedent-setting class action on behalf of fifty thousand educators of color challenging California's teacher certification exam as racially discriminatory; lead counsel defending the landmark decision in Larry P. v. Riles halting California's use of IQ tests with African American special education students; lead counsel in officers for Justice v. City of San Francisco, twenty-five-year effort to integrate the San Francisco Police force; lead counsel in Yvette Doe v. Wilson, challenge which halted Governor Wilson from cutting off prenatal care for seventy thousand undocumented women annually; and cocounsel in Zambrano v. Oakland Unified School District, bilingual education case.

William F. Brazziel, PhD, has been a professor emeritus of higher education, University of Connecticut at Storrs since 1996. He has achieved many honors during his academic career, one of which was director of National Leadership Institute in US Office of Education. He completed research under grants and contracts from the National Institute of Education, National Endowment for the Humanities, National Science Foundation, US Department of Labor, and the Ohio Board of Regents. Author of *Quality Education for All Americans* and coauthor of *Shaping Higher Education's Future*. He has published widely in his field. Correspondence concerning the article "Improving SAT Scores: Pros, Cons, Methods" (included in this volume with his permission) can be addressed to his e-mail Brazziel@Uconnvm.Uconn.edu or fax in 203-423-0127.

Joseph Canton, PhD, received his bachelor of arts degree in sociology from California State University at Los Angeles in 1970, his MA in urban studies in 1971 from Occidental College at Los Angeles, and his PhD in Comparative Cultures from the University of California at Irvine. He is an instructor in the African American Studies Department at City College of San Francisco. Dr. Canton and his wife have a consulting firm that specializes in organization analysis, planning and implementing employee involvement programs, evaluating human resources program effectiveness, and consulting in team building and conflict resolution.

Sandra Cox, PhD received her bachelor of arts degree in history from California State University at Los Angeles, 1967, her MS in educational psychology from the University of Southern California in 1973, and her PhD in education from Claremont Graduate School, Claremont, California, in 1985. Within the Association of Black Psychologists, she has been president of the Los Angeles chapter, Western Regional representative, and chairperson of the National Testing Committee. Currently, she is a school psychologist for the Los Angeles Unified School District and is CEO for the Coalition of Mental Health Professionals, Inc. at Los Angeles.

Harold E. Dent, PhD, received his bachelor of arts degree in psychology from New York University in 1953, his MA in clinical psychology from Denver University, and his PhD in clinical/counseling psychology from the University of Hawaii at Honolulu in 1966. He has published widely in such areas as nondiscriminatory cognitive assessment, cultural/racial bias in test construction, community mental health services administration, and human services delivery systems. He has been director of consultation and education at Westside Community Mental Health Center, San Francisco; director of Outreach Services at the Center for Minority Special Education, Hampton University, Virginia; and coordinator of Pupil Personnel Services, Berkeley Unified School District, Berkeley. Currently, he is an administrator at Shinnecock Indian Reservation, South Hampton, New York.

Vernon G. Gettone, PhD, received his bachelor of arts degree in psychology in 1972 and speech from California State University at San Francisco, his MA in school psychology from the University of California at Berkeley in 1974, and his PhD in school psychology from the University of California at Berkeley in 1976. He is a staff consultant for instruction and professional development at the California Teachers Association at Burlingame, California.

Donald Ross Green, PhD, received his bachelor of arts degree in mathematics at Yale University at New Haven Connecticut and his MA and PhD in education at the University of California at Berkeley. He has teaching experience at Emory University, Atlanta, Georgia, and at the University of California at Berkeley. He has published widely in the area of racial and ethnic test bias. Currently, he is chief research psychologist at CTB/McGraw-Hill, Monterey, California.

Asa Hilliard, EdD, is a professor of educational psychology. Asa Hilliard III was born in Galveston, Texas, on August 22, 1933. After completing high school, Hilliard attended the University of Denver, earning his BA degree in 1955, his MA degree in counseling in 1961, and his EdD degree in educational psychology in 1963. After earning his bachelor's in psychology, Hilliard began teaching in the Denver Public School system, where he remained until 1960; that year, he began as a teaching fellow at the University of Denver, where he remained until he earned his Ph.D.

Joining the faculty at San Francisco State University in 1963, Hilliard spent the next eighteen years there. While at San Francisco State, Hilliard first became department chairman then went on to spend his final eight years as dean of education. Hilliard also served as a consultant to the Peace Corps and as superintendent of schools in Monrovia, Liberia, for two years. Departing from San Francisco State, Hilliard became a professor at Georgia State University; he served as the Fuller E. Callaway Professor of Urban Education, serving in both the Department of Educational Policy Studies and the Department of Educational Psychology and Special Education of Teachers of Education.

William B. Lawson, MD, PhD, received his BS degree from Howard University in 1966, his MA and PhD from the University of New Hampshire in 1969 and 1972, and his MD from Pritzker School of Medicine, University of Chicago in 1978. Currently, he is the chief of Psychiatry and Mental Health, Roudebush, VA Medical Center, Indiana University School of Medicine. He received his diploma from the American Board of Psychiatry and Neurology in 1984. He is former president of the Association of Black Psychiatrists and has published widely in the area of mental health and the black family.

William A. Thomas, PhD, received his bachelor of arts degree in social science from San Francisco State University in 1963, his MA in counseling psychology from San Francisco State University in 1968, and his PhD in counseling psychology from the University of California at Berkeley in 1975. He is a life member of the Association of Black Psychologists and has served as president of the Bay Area Chapter and as Western Regional representative. Currently, he serves as chair of the National Testing Committee. He is a member of the Intelligence Testing Advisory Panel for the State of California; a clinical psychologist who specializes in the assessment and treatment of African American adolescents and their families; and an instructor in African American Studies at City College of San Francisco and adjunct Professor at the California School of Professional Psychology at Alameda, California, where he teaches cognitive assessment. He has appeared on a number of local TV and radio programs pertaining to IQ testing of children.

Robert L. Williams, PhD, received his bachelor of arts degree from Philander Smith College, Little Rock, Arkansas, in 1953; his MEd from Wayne State University; and his PhD from Washington University at St. Louis in 1961. He was one of the founders of the Association of Black Psychologists and served as its second national chairman. Dr. Williams is the developer of the black intelligence test of cultural homogeneity and several other culturally specific tests. Dr. Williams has been a guest on several national television programs relating to IQ testing including CBS's *IQ Myth with Dan Rather, Prime Time Saturday Night, The Phil Donahue Show, Entertainment Television* (BET), and *NBC News* to discuss the controversial topic "Ebonics," a term he coined in 1973. He has published over sixty articles and two books. Currently, he is professor emeritus in Washington University and an elder of elders within the Association of Black Psychologists.

APPENDIX 1

Raising Black Test Scores
Selected Exemplars

William F. Brazziel
Emeritus Professor
University of Higher Education
University of Connecticut

Model Name	Site	Results	Key Person
Curriculum Challenge	Principal borrows curriculum from friend in rich white schools, installs in poor black school.	Test scores rose from 20th to 70th percentile.	Gertrude Williams, Principal Baltimore City Schools
Curriculum Alignment	Consulting firm trains South Carolina teachers and curriculum people to teach more of what is being tested.	Test scores rose from 25th to 60th percentile.	Dr. Vernon Gettone, American Test Service, Columbia, SC
Intensive Reasoning Summer Camps	Washington, DC schools enroll high scoring junior high students in summer camps designed to teach reasoning.	Number of National Merit Scholars increased when students reached junior year in high school.	Washington, DC school superintendent
Intensive Reasoning Courses	University offers intensive reasoning courses designed to prepare Students for entry test to pharmacy and medical school.	School is leading producer in black pharmacists and med-school admissions.	Xavier University of New Orleans. See president and Arthur Whimby, curriculum designer

Number of Black Students Scoring at or Above Selected Points on the 1998 SAT Examination

Point	Number
SAT Total = 900	20,518
SAT Total= 1000	10,665
SAT Total =1100	5,014
SAT Total =1200	2,031

Notes

SAT total represents SAT – V + SAT – M. Note: Scores are pre-recentered scores, i.e., scores before the college board re-centered the test in April of 1995. Recentered scores for black students (and all other students) are higher.

An SAT – T score of 900 in 1995 is equal to 1010 in 1996 in the recentered version of the test, and 1000 is equal to 1100. Accordingly, some 20,000 black test-takers scored 1000 and above on the test in 1996 and well over 2500 scored 1200 and above.

Source of data analysis of SAT Scores for Underrepresented Minority Groups, Marian Brazziel Associates, 1996. For re-centered tables of concordance, see SAT I and SAT II Equivalence Tables, College Entrance Examination Board in 1996.

Note: This analysis was completed by Marian Brazziel Associates (as a subcontractor) under a grant to L. Scott Miller of New Providence, NJ from the EXXON Foundation. Miller is author of an *American Imperative: Accelerating Minority Educational Advancement* by Yale University Press in 1995.

Marian Brazziel Associates
Research, Evaluation, Information Management
42 Beech Mountain Road
Mansfield Center, CT 06250

A Fact Sheet—The Larry P. Case

1. The Larry P. case is a class action suit brought by a group of black parents in San Francisco whose children had been inappropriately classified and placed in classes for the Educable Mentally Retarded (EMR) in the San Francisco Unified School District.

2. The suit was filed in the US District Court for the Northern District of California on November 24, 1971 (no. C-71-2270 FRP), naming as defendants the California State superintendent of Public Instruction, the members of the California State Board of Education, the superintendent of Schools for the San Francisco Unified School District, and the members of the San Francisco Board of Education.

3. The suit contended that the civil rights of the children, guaranteed by the Fourteenth Amendment of the Constitution, had been violated and that they had been denied equal opportunity to education guaranteed by the Civil Rights Act of 1964 and the California Education Code.

4. The plaintiffs alleged:
   A. that their children had been inappropriately classified and placed in EMR classes;
   B. that their children represent a class of "all black children in the state wrongfully labelled and retained in EMR classes";

C.   that the plaintiffs' children and the class they represent had never been mentally retarded but had been wrongfully placed in EMR classes by reason of utilization by school districts throughout the state of standardized IQ tests which fail to account for their (plaintiffs' children) cultural background and home experiences;

D.   that testing procedures are authorized and required by the California State Department of Education; and

E.   that pursuant to the California Education Code (section 6902) such classes should be designed to make EMR students "economically useful and socially adjusted."

5.   The use of culturally biased IQ tests resulted in a disproportionately large number of black children being wrongly labeled mentally retarded and inappropriately placed in EMR classes. For example, in 1969, 28.5 percent of the students enrolled in the San Francisco Unified School District were black, but 58 percent of the students in EMR classes in San Francisco were black. In the same year, 9.1 percent of all students in public schools in the State of California were black, but 27.5 percent of all students in EMR classes in the state were black.

6.   The data for state enrollment in 1973 were essentially the same as they were in 1969, 9 percent of the public school students were black; 25 percent of those in EMR classes were black. However, actual numbers of students in EMR classes in the state had decreased markedly, from almost fifty-five thousand in 1969 to thirty-four thousand in 1973. The proportions remained the same.

7.   At the other end of the continuum, there was a disproportionately small number of black children enrolled in the classes for Mentally Gifted Minors (MGM). In 1969, the State Department of Education reported only 2.5 percent of the children in MGM classes were black, yet 9 percent of the children in public schools were black.

8. On June 21, 1972, Judge Robert F. Peckham issued a preliminary injunction against the San Francisco Unified School District to enjoin the district from requiring the use of IQ tests that do not account for the cultural and experiential background of black children.

9. The San Francisco Unified School District appealed that injunction. In August 1973, the Ninth Circuit Court of Appeals upheld Peckham's decision.

10. The plaintiffs went back to court and asked Judge Peckham to extend his injunction to the State of California on behalf of all black children inappropriately placed in EMR classes.

11. On December 14, 1974, Judge Peckham extended the class of children to include all black children in the State of California (inappropriately classified EMR) and enjoined the state from requiring the use of culturally biased IQ tests for the purpose of placing black children in EMR classes.

12. At its December 1974 meeting, the California State Board of Education declared a moratorium on the use of IQ tests on all children being considered for EMR placement.

13. The Larry P. trial began October 11, 1977, and final arguments were heard on May 30, 1978. Among the witnesses for the plaintiffs were ABPsi members Asa Hilliard, EdD; Reginald Jones, PhD; Gerald West, PhD; William Pierce, PhD; and Harold Dent, PhD. Other expert witnesses called by plaintiffs included Gloria Powell, MD; Alice Watkins, PhD; Jane Mercer, PhD; George Albee, PhD; and Leon Kamin, PhD.

14. Defense witnesses included Lloyd Humphreys, PhD; Nadine Lambert, PhD; Robert Thorndike, PhD; Leo Munday, PhD; and Jerome Doppelt, PhD.

15. Almost a year and half after closing arguments, October 16, 1979, Judge Peckham issued his landmark decision (no. C71-2270 RFP). The court found:
    A. that federal and state constitutional law and federal statutory law had been violated (the Civil Rights Act of 1964, Section 504 of the Rehabilitation Act of 1973

and the Education for all Handicapped Children's Act of 1975);

B. that IQ tests were culturally biased and had not been validated for the purpose for which they were being used—placement of black children in EMR classes;

C. that the plaintiffs' constitutional rights to equal education had been violated by wrongfully confining them to "dead-end" EMR classes;

D. that the plaintiffs' constitutional guarantees of equal protection by the laws had been violated by the State's "unjustified toleration of disproportionate enrollments of black children in EMR classes, and the use of placement mechanisms, particularly IQ tests, that perpetuate those disproportions..." (3); and

E. that "defendants' conduct, in connection with the history of IQ testing and special education in California, reveals an unlawful segregative intent. This intent was not necessarily to hurt black children, but it was an intent to assign a grossly disproportionate number of black children to the special EMR classes, and it was manifested, inter alia, in the use of invalidated and racially and culturally biased placement criteria" (3–4).

16. The court ordered the following injunctive relief:

A. "Defendants are enjoined from utilizing, permitting the use of, or approving the use of any standardized intelligence test...for the identification of black RIVER children or their placement into EMR classes without securing approval of the court" (104).

B. "Defendants are hereby ordered to monitor and eliminate disproportionate placement of black children in California's EMR classes" (105).

C. "To remedy the harm to black children who have been misidentified as EMR pupils and to prevent these discriminatory practices from recurring in California with respect to a similarly situated class of youngsters in the future, the defendants shall direct each school district to reevaluate every black child currently identified as an EMR pupil without including in the psychological evaluation a standardized intelligence or ability test, that has not been approved by the court..." (106–107).

17. In December 1979, the California State Board of Education voted not to appeal the Larry P. decision.

18. Wilson Riles, then State superintendent of Public Instruction, did appeal the Larry P. decision.

19. On January 23, 1984, the US Court of Appeals for the Ninth Circuit affirmed the district court's findings of violation of federal statutes but found it unnecessary to reach federal constitutional issues. The appellate court also affirmed the findings of violation of California's constitutional equal protection provision.

20. The State Department of Education filed a petition for rehearing en banc (rehearing by the entire bench; that is, a rehearing by all twenty-nine judges of the appellate court).

21. On June 25, 1986, the appellate court issued an amended decision which:
    A. denied the petition for rehearing;
    B. rejected the motion for an en banc review;
    C. reaffirmed the district court findings of violation of federal statutory law and the required remedy; and
    D. reversed the finding of violations of federal and state constitutional law.

22. In December 1986, in light of the Ninth Circuit's affirmance and substantial modifications to the California special education system—most notably, the elimination of the label, EMR—the State Department of Education and the Larry P. plaintiffs reached a settlement concerning implementation of the 1979 injunction. The parties stipulated to elimination of IQ testing for all African American pupils being considered for special education inasmuch as former EMR students could be found eligible for special education

under virtually any of the newly devised labels and placed in virtually any of the newly structured placements.

23. In May 1988, a group of African American plaintiffs, represented by the conservative public interest group, the Landmark Legal foundation from Missouri, filed a legal challenge to the 1986 settlement, Crawford v. Honig. The plaintiffs claimed that they had a constitutional right to IQ tests which they believed benefitted their education. They also contended they had not had notice or an opportunity to contest the 1986 settlement in accord with constitutional due process requirements.

24. The Crawford v. Honig case was transferred to Northern California and consolidated with the Larry P. case. In September 1992, the same district court judge who had issued the Larry P. decision issued an order vacating the 1986 settlement on the constitutional due process grounds. The court did not decide whether plaintiffs' constitutional rights were violated in being denied access to IQ tests. The court denied plaintiffs motion to make their case a class action and allowed, in effect, one African American student to take an IQ test. In place of the 1986 settlement, the court invited the parties to return to court to determine the current "substantial equivalent" of the prior EMR category so as to determine the current proper scope of the 1979 order. The court acknowledged the results of that inquiry could be as broad or broader than the original 1979 injunction.

25. The Larry P. plaintiffs and the State Department of Education appealed the district court's ruling. On January 6, 1995, the US Court of Appeals for the Ninth Circuit affirmed the lower court's determination to vacate the 1986 settlement but left intact the original 1979 injunction in Larry P.

26. On September 10, 1992, the State Department of Education instructed school districts to continue not to use IQ tests when identifying and placing African American

students in special education, pending new court hearings to determine the current "substantial equivalent" of the prior EMR category.

REFERENCES

Introduction

Barnes, Edward J. 1972. "Cultural Retardation or Shortcomings of Assessment Techniques." *Black Psychology*, edited by Reginald L. Jones. New York: Harper and Row.

Katz, Irwin. 1964. "Review of Evidence Relating to Effects of Desegregation on Intellectual Performances of Negroes." *American Psychologist.* 19:381–389.

Katz, Irwin, James M. Robinson, Edgar G. Epps, and Patricia Waly. 1964. "Race of Experimenter and Instruction in the Expression of Hostility by Negro Boys." *Journal of Social Issues.* 20:54–60.

Thomas, William A. 1975. "Using Peer Counseling to Reduce Interference and Improve the Academic Achievement of School Children." Unpublished doctoral dissertation. University of California, Berkeley.

Williams, Robert L. 1971. "Abuses and Misuses in Testing Black Children." *The Counseling Psychologist.* 2:62–73.

Suggested Readings

Barnes, Julian E. 1970. "A Surprising Turn on Minority Enrollments." *US News and World Report*, Vol. 123. No. 25, 34–35.

Brazziel, William F. 1988. "Improving SAT Scores: Pros, Cons, Methods." *Journal of Negro Education*, Vol. 57. No. 1, 81–93.

Bronner, Ethan. 1997. "Colleges Look for Answers to Racial Gaps in Testing." *The New York Times*, Vol. CXLVII, 1.

Dent, Harold E. 1987. "The Larry P. case: A Fact Sheet." *Negro Educational Review*, Vol. 34, 192–95.

Eyde, Lorraine D. et.al. 1993. *Responsible Test Use: American Psychological Association*. Washington, D.C.

Hilliard, Asa. 1995. "Either a Paradigm Shift or No Mental Measurement." *Psych Discourse*, Vol. 26, No. 10, 6–20.

Hilliard, Asa G. III. 1976. "Alternatives to IQ testing: An approach to the identification of 'gifted' minority children." Final report to the California State Department of Education, Special Education Support Unit, ERIC Clearinghouse on Early Childhood Education, ED 146-009.

Kamin L. 1974. *The Science and Politics of IQ*. New York. John Wiley

Lezak, Muriel D. 1988. "IQ: R.I.P." *Journal of Clinical and Experimental Neuropsychology*, Vol. 10 No. 3, 351–361.

Mitchell, Horace. 1975. "Testing and Student Classification." *Conference Proceedings, Desegregation and Beyond: The Educational and Legal Issues*. The University of Michigan. Ann Arbor, 76–81.

Neisser, Ulric, et al. 1996. "Intelligence: Knowns and Unknowns." *American Psychologist*, Vol. 51. No. 2, 77–101.

Romney, Lee. 2019. "A Legacy of Mistreatment for San Francisco's Black special education students." https://www.kalw.org/post/legacy-mistreatment-san-francisco-s-black-special-ed-students

Thomas, William A. 1997. "Position Statement on Intelligence Testing." *Psych Discourse*, Vol. 28, No. 9, 13.

Williams, Robert F. and Wendell Rivers. 1975. "The Effects of Language on the Test Performance of Black Children." *Ebonics: The True Language of Black Folks*, edited by Robert L. Williams, 96–109.

Williams, Robert F. 1972. "The Bitch-100: A Culture-Specific Test." A paper presented at the Annual Meeting of the American Psychological Association. Honolulu, Hawaii.

Williams, Wendy and Stephen J. Ceci. 1997. "Are Americans Becoming More or Less Alike?" *American Psychologist* Vol. 52, No. 11, 1235–1236.

Chapter 1

Galton F. 1869. *Hereditary Genetics: An Inquiry Into Its Laws and Consequences*. London: MacMillan.

Gould, S. J. 1981. *The Mismeasure of Man*. New York: W.W.

Hilliard, A. G. 1995. "Either a paradigm shift or no mental measurement." *Psych Discourse*, 26, 6–20.

Humphreys, L. G. 1971. *Theory of Intelligence: In R. Cancro (Ed.) Intelligence, Genetics, and Environmental Influences*. New York: Grune and Stratton, 31–55.

Jensen, A. R. 1980. *Bias in Mental Testing*. New York: The Free Press.

Jensen, A. R. 1969. "How much can we boost IQ and scholastic achievement?" *Harvard Educational Review*, 39, 1–123.

Kamin, L. 1974. *Science and Politics of IQ*. New York.

Norton. Herrnstein, R. 1971. "IQ." *Atlantic Monthly* (September): 43–64.

Rushton, J. P. 1995. *Race, Evolution, and Behavior: A Life History Perspective*. New Brunswick, New Jersey: Transaction Books.

Terman, L. M. 1916. *The Measurement of Intelligence*. Boston: Houghton-Mifflin.

Wechsler, D.(1958. *Measurement of Adult Intelligence* (3rd ed.) Baltimore: Williams and Wilkins.

Wesman, A. G. 1968. "Intelligence testing." *American Psychologist*, 23, 267–271.

Wiley, John, C. Murray, and R. Herrnstein. 1994. *The Bell Curve: Intelligence and Class Structure in American Life*. New York: Free Press.

Williams, R. L. 1974. "History of the Association of Black Psychologists: early formation and development." *Journal of Black Psychology*, 1, 9–24.

Williams, R. L. 1974. "Scientific Racism and IQ: the Silent Mugging of the Black Community." *Psychology Today* (May) 32–41.

Williams, R. L. 1972. "The BITCH TEST: A culture specific test." A paper presented at the annual convention of the American Psychological Association. Honolulu, Hawaii.

Williams, R. L. 1997. "The Ebonics Controversy." *Journal of Black Psychology*, 23, 208–214.

Williams, R. L. and L. W. Rivers. 1972. "The use of standard and nonstandard English in testing black children." A paper presented at the annual meeting of the American Psychological Association. Honolulu, Hawaii.

Williams, R. L. 1999. "The purposes and missions of ABPsi: open letter to the president of the American Psychological Association." *Psych Discourse*, 30, 3–6.

Chapter 2

Alleyne, M. C. 1980. *Comparative Afro-American*. Ann Arbor: Karoma Publishers.

Angoff, W. H. 1971. *Scales, norms, and equivalent scores. In R. L. Thorndike (Ed.), Educational measurement*. Washington, D. C.: American Council on Education.

Bever, T. G. 1972. *Perceptions, thought, and language. In J. B. Carroll and R. 0. Freedle (Eds.) Language, comprehension, and the acquisition of knowledge*. Washington, D.C.: Winston, 99–112.

Cole, M., and S. Scribner. 1973. *Culture and thought*. New York: Wiley.

Crawford v. Honig Case No. C-89-0014 RFP.

Crawford v. Honig 33F. 3d 485 (9th Circ. 1994).

Cronbach, L. J. C., and P. J. D. Drenth (Eds.) 1972. *Mental tests and cultural adaptations*. Paris: Mouton.

Feuerstein, R. 1980. *Instrumental enrichment*. Baltimore: University Park Press.

Feuerstein, R. 1979. *The dynamic assessment of retarded performers*. Baltimore: University Park Press.

Freire, P. 1973. *Education for critical consciousness*. New York: Seabury.

Fuller, R. 1977. *In search of the IQ correlation*. Stonybrook, New York: Ball-Stick-Bird Publications.

Grady, John F. 1980. *Parents in Action on Special Education (PASE)*, an incorporated Association; Lue B. on her own behalf and as the next friend of Barbara B.; and Onollie J., on her own behalf and as the next friend of Angela J., on behalf of themselves and all other persons similarly situated, Plaintiffs, v. Joseph P. Hannon, individually and in his capacity as General Superintendent of Schools in Chicago et al. No. 74C3586, in the Northern United States District Court for the Northern District of Illinois, Eastern Division.

Hall, E.T. 1977. *Beyond culture*. New York: Anchor.

Hilliard, A. G. 1995. "Either a Paradigm Shift or No Mental Measurement." *Psych Discourse*, vs. 26, No.10, 8–20.

Hilliard, A. G. 1981. "I.Q. thinking as catechism: Ethnic and cultural bias or invalid science." *Black Books Bulletin*, 7(2), 99–112.

Holtzman, W. H., K. Heller and S. Messick (Eds.). 1980. *Placing children in special education: A strategy for equity*. Washington, D.C.: National Academy Press.

Jensen, A. 1980. *Bias in mental testing*. New York: Free Press.

Kamin, L. 1974. *The science and politics of IQ*. New York: Wiley.

Larry P. v. Riles 495 F. Supp. 926 (N.D. Cal. 1979).

Larry P. v. Lucille P. vs. Riles 793 F 2nd 969 (9th Circ. 1984), amended (9th Circ. 1986). *The Journal of Black Psychology* August 1983, Vol. 10, No, 1, Pp. 1–18.

Mandler, J. M., and N. L. Stein. "The myth of perceptual defect: Sources and evidence." Unpublished manuscript. University of California at San Diego and Washington University.

Orasanu, J., R. P. MacDennott, and A. W. Boykin. 1977. *A critique of test standardization Social policy*. September/October. 61–67.

Peckham, R. F. and Larry P. by his guardian ad litem, Lucille P. et al., Plaintiffs, Wilson Riles, Superintendent of Public Instruction for the State of California et al. Defendants, in the United States District Court for the Northern District of California No. C-71-2270RFP, 1979.

Peckham, R. F. and Larry P., by his guardian ad litem, Lucille P.; M. S., by his guardian ad litem, Joyce S.; M. J., by his guardian ad litem, Theresa J.; John, by his guardian a, litem, Mary H., Sylvia M., by her guardian ad litem, Sylvia W.; R. L., by his guardian: ad litem, Salina F., Plaintiffs-Appellees, v. Wilson Riles,

Superintendent of Public Instruction for the State of California, Defendant-Appellant, Henry P. Gunderson, e al. Defendants. Court of Appeals Docket No. 80-4027, Appellant's Opening Brief United States Court of Appeals for the Ninth Circuit, 1981.

Rand Y., A. J. Tannenbaum, and R. Feuerstein. 1979. "Effects of instrumental enrichment on the psychoeducational development of low-functioning adolescents." *Journal Educational Psychology*, 71(6), 751–762.

Shuy, R. 1977. *Quantitative language data: A case for and some warnings against Anthropology and Education Quarterly.* 1 (2), 78–82.

Smith, E. 1978. "The retention of the phonological, phonemic, and morphophonemic, features of Africa in Afro-American ebonies." Fullerton, Calif.: Seminar Series Paper Department of Linguistics, California State University at Fullerton.

Stewart, M. 1981. "Melanin and sensory-motor intelligence." Doctoral dissertation, Georgi Peabody College of Education, Vanderbilt University.

Tryon, W. W. 1979. "The test-trait fallacy." *American Psychologist.* 4(5), 402–406.

Turner, L. D. 1969. *Africanisms in the Gullah dialect.* New York: Arnold Press.

Valentine, C. A., and B. Valentine. 1975. "Brain damage and the intellectual defense on inequality." *Current Anthropology*, March 16(1), 117–150.

Vass, W. K. 1979. *The Bantu-speaking heritage of the United States. Los Angeles: Center for Afro-American Studies.* University of California.

Wigdor, A. K., and W. K. Garner (Eds.). 1982. *Ability testing: Consequences and controversy.* Washington, D.C.: National Academy Press.

Chapter 3

Baclder, A. and S. Eakin, (Eds.). 1993. *Every child can succeed: Readings for school improvement.* Bloomington, IN: Agency for Instructional Technology.

Cole, M., J. Gay, J. A. Glick, D. W. Sharp, et al. 1971. *The cultural context of learning and thinking: An exploration in experimental anthropology.* New York: Basic Books.

Dent, H. E. 1991. "The San Francisco Public Schools experience with alternatives to IQ testing: A model for non-biased assessment." In A. G. Hilliard Ill (F.d.), *Testing African American students* (146–162). Morristown, NJ: Aaron.

Duke, L. 1991. "Whites racial stereotyping persists: Most retain negative beliefs about minorities, survey finds." *The Washington Post*, A 1.

Edmonds, R. R. 1979. "Some schools work and more can." *Social Policy.* 28–32.

Fairchild, H. H. 1991. "Scientific racism: The cloak of objectivity." *Journal of Social Issues*, 47(3), 101–115.

Feuerstein, R. 1979. *The dynamic assessment of retarded performers: The learning potential assessment device.* Baltimore, MD: University Park.

Feuerstein, R. 1980. *Instrumental enrichment.* Baltimore, MD: University Park.

Feuerstein, R., P.S. Klein, and A. J. Tannenbaum. 1991. *Mediated Learning experience (MLE) theoretical, psychological and learning implications.* London: Freund.

Fuller, R. 1977. *In search of the IQ correlation: A scientific whodunit.* Stony Brook, NY: Ball-Stick-Bird.

Gardner, H. 1983. *Frames of mind: The theory of multiple intelligences.* London: Paladin.

Glass, G. V. 1983. "Effectiveness of special education." *Policy Studies Review*, 2(1). University of Kansas.

Gould, S. 1981. *The mis measure of man.* New York: Norton.

Guthrie, R. 1976. *Even the rat was white.* New York: Harper & Row.

Hall, E.T. 1977. *Beyond culture.* New York: Anchor.

Hehir, T., and T. Latus (Eds.). 1993. *Special education at the century's end: Evolution of theory and practice since 1970* (Reprint Series No. 23). Cambridge, MA: Harvard Educational Review.

Heller, K. A., W. H. Holtzman, and S. Messick. 1982. *Placing children in special education: A strategy for equity.* Washington, DC: National Academy Press.

Helms, J. E. 1992. "Why is there no study of cultural equivalence in standardized cognitive ability testing?" *American Psychologist*, 47(9), 1083–1101.

Hilliard, A.G. III. 1987. "The learning potential assessment device and instrumental enrichment as a paradigm shift." *Negro Educational Review*, 38(2-3), 200–208.

Hilliard, A.G. III. (Ed). 1987. "Testing African American students" [Special issue]. *Negro Educational Review*, 38 (2–3).

Hilliard, A.G. III. 1990. "Back to Binet: The case against the use of IQ tests in the schools." *Contemporary Education*, 61(4), 184–189.

Holtzman. W. H. 1982. "Preface." In K. A. Heller, W. H. Holtzman, and S. Messick (Eds.). *Placing children in special education: A strategy for equity.* Washington, DC: National Academy Press.

Hoover, M. R., R. L. Politzer, and O. Taylor. 1991. "Bias in reading tests for Black language speakers: A sociolinguistic perspective." In A.G. Hilliard III (Ed.), *Testing African American students* (81–98). Moristown, NJ: Aaron.

Jensen, A. 1980. *Bias in mental testing.* New York: Free Press.

Jensen, A. 1969. "How much can we boost IQ?" *Harvard Educational Review*.

Jensen, M. R. 1992. "Principles of change models in schools psychology and education." In *Advances in cognition and educational practice* (Vol. 18, 47–72). Greenwich, CT: Jai.

Kamin, L. 1974. *The science and politics of IQ.* New York: Wiley.

Kluwe, R. H., C. Misiak, and H. Haider. 1991. "The control of complex systems and performance in intelligence tests." In *H.A.H. Rowe (Ed.), Intelligence, reconceptualization and measurement. Australian Council for Educational Research.* Hillsdale, NJ: Lawrence Erlbaum.

Kozol, J. 1991. *Savage inequalities: Children in America's schools.* New York: Crown.

Lidz, C. S. 1991. *Practitioner's guide to dynamic assessment.* New York: Guilford.

Montagu, A. 1974. *Man's most dangerous myth: The fallacy of race.* New York.

Richele, M. N. 1991. "Reconciling views on intelligence." In *H.A.H. Rowe (Ed.), Intelligence, reconceptualization and measurement. Australian Council for Educational Research.* Hillsdale, NJ: Lawrence Erlbaum.

Rowe, H. A. H. (Ed.). 1991. "Intelligence, reconceptualization and measurement." *Australian Council for Educational Research.* Hillsdale, NJ: Lawrence Erlbaum.

Shuy, R. W. 1977. *Quantitative linguistic analysis: A case for and some warnings against Anthropology and Education Quarterly,* 1(2), 78–82.

Sizemore, B. 1988. *The algebra of African-American achievement. Effective Schools: Critical Issues in the Education of Black Children.* 123–149. (Washington, DC: National Alliance of Black School Educators)

Skyrtic, T. M. 1991. "The special education paradox: F. equity as the way to excellence." *Harvard Educational Review,* 61(2), 148–206.

Smith, E. A. 1978. "The retention of the phonological, phonemic, and morphophonemic features of Africa in Afro-American ebonies." *Seminar Series Paper,* No. 40. Fullerton: California State University at Fullerton, Department of Linguistics.

Smith, E. A. 1979. "A diagnostic instrument/or assessing the phonological competence and performance of the inner-city Afro-American child." *Seminar Series Paper,* No. 41. Fullerton: California State University at Fullerton, Department of Linguistics.

Snyderman, M. and S. Rothman. 1990. *The I.Q. controversy: The media and public policy.* New Brunswick, NJ: Transaction.

Suzuki, S. 1984. *Nurtured by love: The classic approach to talent education.* Smithtown, NY: Exposition.

Yee, A. H. 1983. "Ethnicity and race: Psychological perspectives." *Educational Psychologist*, 18(1), 14–24.

Zacharias, J. R. 1977. "The trouble with tests." In P. L. Houts (Ed.), *The myth of measurability*. New York: Hart.

Additional Reading

Baller, W. R., D. C. Charles, and E. L. Miller. 1967. "Mid-life attainment of the mentally retarded: A longitudinal study." *Genetic Psychology Monographs*, 75, 235–329.

Bower, B. 1992. "Infants signal the birth of knowledge." *Science News*, 142(20), 325.

Bruer, J. T. 1993. "The mind's journey from novice to expert: If we know the route, we can help students negotiate their way." *American Educator*, 6–46.

Chase, A. 1977. *The legacy of Malthus: The social cost of scientific racism*. New York: Alfred A. Knopf.

Chomsky, N. 1971. "Deep structure, surface structure, and semantic interpretation." In D. Steinberg and L. Jalcobovitz (Eds.), *Semantics*. New York: Cambridge University Press.

Cohen, R. 1969. "Conceptual styles, culture conflict, and non-verbal tests of intelligence." *American Anthropologist*, 71 (5), 828–857.

Cohen, R. 1971. "The influence of conceptual rule sets on measures of learning ability." In *Race and Intelligence. Anthropological Association*.

Dillon, R., and R. J. Sternberg. 1986. *Cognition and instruction*. New York: Academic Press.

Donaldson, M. 1978. *Children's minds*. New York: Norton.

Ginsburg, H. 1972. *The myth of the deprived child: Poor children's intellect*. Englewood Cliffs, NJ: Prentice-Hall.

Hilliard, A. G. III. 1976. "Alternatives to IQ testing: An approach to the identification of 'gifted' minority children." Final report to the California State Department of Education, Special Education Support Unit (ERIC Clearinghouse on Early Childhood Education, ED 146-009)

Hilliard, A.G. 1981. "IQ thinking as catechism: Ethnic and cultural bias or invalid science." *Black Books Bulletin*, 7(2), 99–112

Hilliard, A. G. III. 1984. "IQ thinking as the emperor's new clothes." In C. Reynolds and R. T. Brown (Eds.), *Perspectives on bias in mental testing* (139–169). New York: Plenum.

Hilliard, A. G. III. 1983. "Psychological factors associated with language in the education of the African-American child." *Journal of Negro education*, 52(1), 24–34.

Hilliard, A. G. III. 1990. "Misunderstanding and testing intelligence." In J. Goodlad and P. Keating (Eds.), *Access to knowledge: An agenda/or our nation's schools*. New York: College Board.

Hilliard, A. G., III. 1979. "The pedagogy of success." In *The most enabling environment*. Washington, DC: Association for Early Childhood International.

Hilliard, A. G. 1994. "Thinking skills and students placed at greatest risk in the educational system." In *Restructuring learning: 1990 Summer Institute Papers and Recommendations* (147–186). Washington, DC: Council of Chief State School Officers.

Jacobs, P. 1977. *Up the IQ*. New York: Wyden.

Labov, W. 1970. "The logic of non-standard English." In F. Williams (Ed.), *Language and poverty*. Chicago: Markham.

Lidz, C. S. (Eds.). 1987. *Dynamic assessment: An international approach to evaluating learning potential*. New York: Guilford.

Lipsky, D. K., and A. Gartner. 1989. *Beyond separate education: Quality education/or all*. Baltimore: Paul ff. Brookes.

Oakes, J. 1985. *Keeping How schools structure inequality*. New Haven, CT: Yale University Press.

Slack, W. V. and D. Porter. 1980. "The Scholastic Aptitude Test: A critical appraisal." *Harvard Educational Review*, 50(2), 154–178.

Spitz, H. H. 1986. *The raising of intelligence: A selected history of attempts to raise retarded intelligence*. Hillsdale, NJ: Lawrence Erlbaum.

Wigdor, A. K., and W. K. Gamer (Eds.). 1982. *Ability testing: Uses, consequences, and controversy*. Washington, DC: National Academy Press.

Wiggins, G. P. 1993. *Assessing student performance: Exploring the purpose and limits of testing.* San Francisco: Jossey-Bass.

Chapter 4

Anastasi, A. 1968. *Psychological Testing* (3rd ed.) New York: Macmillian.

Angelino, H., and C. L. Shedd. 1955. "An initial report of a validation study of the Davis-Eells Test of General Intelligence or Problem Solving Ability." *Journal of Psychology.* 40, 35–38.

Angoff, W. H. and S. F. Ford. 1971. "Item-race interaction on a test of scholastic aptitude." *College Entrance Examination Board Research and Development Reports.* RB 71–59.

Brown, W. M. and R. D. Russell. 1964. "Limitation of admissions testing for the disadvantaged (letter)." *The Personnel and Guidance Journal,* 43, 301–304.

Cardall, C. and W. E. Coffman. 1964. "A method for comparing the performance of different groups on the items in a test." *College Entrance Examination Board Research and Development Reports.* RB 9.

Chang, S. S. and J. Raths. 1971. "The schools' contribution to the cumulating deficit." *The Journal of Educational Research.* 64, 272–276.

Cleary, T. A. 1968. "Test bias: prediction of grades of Negro and white students in integrated colleges." *Journal of Educational Measurement.* 5, 115–124.

Cleary, T. A. and T. L. Hilton. 1968. "An investigation of item bias." *Educational and Psychological Measurement.* 28, 61–75.

Coleman, J. S. et al. 1966. *Equality of Educational Opportunity.* US Department of Health, Education, and Welfare.

Darlington, R. B. 1971. "Another look at 'culture fairness.'" *Journal of Educational Measurement.* 8, 71–82.

Davis, J. A. and G. Temp. 1971. "Is the SAT biased against black students?" *College Board Review.* 2–9.

Eells, K., Al Davis, R. J. Havinghurst, V. E. Herrick, and R. W. Tyler. 1951. *Intelligence and cultural differences.* Chicago: University of Chicago Press.

Gilbert, H. B. 1966. "On the IQ ban." *Teachers College Record.* 67, 282–285.

Green, D. R. 1971. "Biased tests." (unpublished manuscript).

Green, R. L. and W. W. Farquhar. 1965. "Negro academic motivation and scholastic achievement." *Journal of Educational Psychology.* 56, 241–243.

Hewer, V. H. 1965. "Are tests fair to college students from homes with low socio-economic status?" *Personnel and Guidance Journal.* 43, 764–769.

Houston, S. 1971. "Cultural disadvantages: creativity, cooperation." *Behavior Today.* 2, (24), 3.

Hunter, L. B. and F. A. Rogers. 1967. "Testing: politics and pretense." *The Urban Review,* 2 (3), 5–6, 8, 25–26.

Jensen, A. R. 1968. "How Much can we boost 10 and scholastic achievement?" *Harvard Educational Review,* 39, 1–123.

Kennedy, W. A., Van De Reit, and J. C. White. 1963. "A normative sample of intelligence and achievement of Negro elementary school children in the southeastern United States." *Monographs of the Society for Research in Child Development.* 28, No. 6.

Lesser, G. S., G. Fifer, and D. H. Clark. 1965. "Mental abilities of children from different social-class and cultural groups." *Monographs of the Society for Research in Child Development,* 30 (4, Whole No. 102).

Linn, R. L. and C. E. Werts. 1971. "Considerations for studies of test bias." *Journal of Educational Measurement.* 8, 1–4.

Lord, FM. and M. R. Novick. 1968. "Statistical theories of mental test scores." Reading, Mass: Addison-Wesley.

Lorge, I. 1966. "Difference or bias in tests of intelligence." In A. Anastasi (Ed.) *Testing problems in perspective.* Washington, D.C.: American Council on Education. 456–471.

Mercer, J. R. 1971. "Pluralistic diagnosis in the evaluation of black and Chicano children." Paper presented at the American Psychological Association, Washington, D.C. September.

Merz, W. R. 1970. "A factor analysis of the Goodenough-Harris Drawing Test across four ethnic groups." *Dissertation Abstracts International.* 31, 1627 A.

Messick, S., and S. Anderson. 1970. "Educational testing, individual development, and social responsibility." *The Counseling Psychologist.* 2, 80–88.

Potthoff, R. F. 1966. "Statistical aspects of the problem of biases in psychological tests." *University of North Carolina Institute of Statistics Mimeo Series.* No. 479.

Ruch, G. M. 1929. *The objective or new-type examination.* Chicago: Scott, Foresman and Co.

Stanley, J.C. and A. C. Porter. 1967. "Correlation of Scholastic Aptitude Test scores with college grades for Negroes versus whites." *Journal of Educational Measurement.* 4, 199–218.

Terman, L. M. 1916. *The measurement of Intelligence.* Boston: Houghton Mifflin.

Terman, L. M. and M. A. Merrill. 1960. *Stanford-Binet Intelligence Scale: Manual for the Third Revision, Form L-M.* Boston-Houghton Mifflin.

Thornclike, R. L. 1971. "Concepts of culture-fairness." *Journal of Educational Measurement.* 8, 63–70.

Wasserman, M. 1969. "Planting pansies on the roof." *The Urban Review.* 3 (3), 30–35.

Williams, R. L. 1970. "Black pride, academic relevance and individual achievement." *The Counseling Psychologist.* 18–22.

Chapter 5

Campbell, P. 1992. Criterion assessment Paper presented at Advisory Committee Meeting on Reform in California Assessment, Sacramento, CA.

Canton, Joseph. 1976. "Total Personnel Assessment: A Case Study in Affirmative Action—City of Santa Ana, California." Unpublished

Dent, H. E. 1996. "Non-biased assessment or realistic assessment." In R.L. Jones (Ed.) *The handbook of tests and measurements for black populations* (102–122). Cobb and Henry, Berkeley, CA.

Dent, H. E. 1991. The Larry P. project in assessment and curriculum (Contract No. 8283). Final report of the California Department of Education, Sacramento, CA.

Figeroa, R. A. 1984. "The non-psychometric assessment of children's intelligence." Unpublished manuscript. University of California, Davis.

Green, D. R. 1972. "Racial and ethnic bias in test construction" (Contract No. OEC9-70-0058571). Final report of the US Office of Education, Washington, D.C.

Haywood, H. C. and D. Tzuriel. 1992. *Interactive assessment.* New York: Springer-Verlag.

Larry P v. Riles (1979) 495 F. Supp. Northern District, California.

Larry P et al. v. Wilson Riles et. al. C-71-2270 RFP (ND Cal. 1979) Aft'd 793 F. 2nd 979 (9th Cir.) January 23, 1984, as Amended, June 25, 1986).

Lidz, C. S. 1987. *Dynamic assessment: an international approach to evaluating learning potential.* New York: Guilford.

Sternberg, R. J. (Ed.). 1982. *Handbook of human intelligence.* Cambridge University Press.

Taylor, D. 1992. Authentic assessment Paper presented at Advisory Committee on Reform of California Assessment, Sacramento, CA.

Tucker, J. A. (Ed.). 1985. "Curriculum-based assessment." (Special Issue). *Exceptional Children.* 52 (3).

Ysseldyke, J. E. and R. R. Regan. 1980. "Non-discriminatory assessment: A formative model." *Exceptional Children.* 46, 465–466.

Chapter 6

Alleyne, M. C. 1980. *Comparative Afro-American.* Ann Arbor: Karoma Publishers.

Angoff, W. H. 1971. "Scales, norms, and equivalent scores." In R. L. Thorndike (Ed.), *Educational measurement*. Washington, D. C.: American Council on Education.

Bever, T. G. 1972. "Perceptions, thought, and language." In J. B. Carroll and R. O. Freedle (Eds.) *Language, comprehension, and the acquisition of knowledge*. Washington, D.C.: Winston. 99–112.

Cole, M. and S. Scribner. 1973. *Culture and thought*. New York: Wiley.

Cronbach, L. J. C. and P. J. D. Drenth (Eds.). 1972. *Mental tests and cultural adaptations*. Paris: Mouton, 1972.

Feuerstein, R. 1980. *Instrumental enrichment*. Baltimore: University Park Press.

Feuerstein, R. 1979. *The dynamic assessment of retarded performers*. Baltimore: University Park Press.

Freire, P. 1973. *Education for critical consciousness*. New York: Seabury.

Fuller, R. 1977. *In search of the IQ correlation*. Stonybrook, New York: Ball-Stick-Bird Publications.

Grady, John F. 1980. Parents in Action on Special Education (PASE), an incorporated Association; Lue B. on her own behalf and as the next friend of Barbara B.; and Onollie J., on her own behalf and as the next friend of Angela J., on behalf of themselves and all other persons similarly situated, Plaintiffs, v. Joseph P. Hannon, individually and in his capacity as General Superintendent of Schools in Chicago et al. No. 74C3586, in the Northern United States District Court for the Northern District of Illinois, Eastern Division.

Hall, E. T. 1977. *Beyond culture*. New York: Anchor.

Hilliard, A. G. 1981. "I.Q. thinking as catechism: Ethnic and cultural bias or invalid science." *Black Books Bulletin*. 7(2), 99–112.

Holtzman, W. H., K. Heller, and S. Messick. (Eds.). 1980. *Placing children in special education: A strategy for equity*. Washington, D.C.: National Academy Press, 1980.

Jensen, A. 1980. *Bias in mental testing*. New York: Free Press.

Kamin, L. 1974. *The science and politics of IQ*. New York: Wiley.

Mandler, J. M. and N. L. Stein. "The myth of perceptual defect: Sources and evidence." Unpublished manuscript. University of California at San Diego and Washington University.

Orasanu, J., R. P. MacDennott, and A. W. Boykin. 1977. *A critique of test standardization Social policy.* September/October, 61–67.

Peckham, R. F. 1979. Larry P. by his guardian ad litem, Lucille P. et al., Plaintiffs, Wilson Riles, Superintendent of Public Instruction for the State of California et al. Defendants, in the United States District Court for the Northern District of California No. C-71-2270RFP.

Peckham, R. F. 1981. Larry P., by his guardian ad litem, Lucille P.; M. S., by his guardian ad litem, Joyce S.; M. J., by his guardian ad litem, Theresa J.; John, by his guardian a, litem, Mary H., Sylvia M., by her guardian ad litem, Sylvia W.; R. L., by his guardian: ad litem, Salina F., Plaintiffs-Appellees, v. Wilson Riles, Superintendent of Public Instruction for the State of California, Defendant-Appellant, Henry P. Gunderson, e al. Defendants. Court of Appeals Docket No. 80-4027, Appellant's Opening Brief United States Court of Appeals for the Ninth Circuit.

Rand Y., A. J. Tannenbaum, and R. Feuerstein. 1979. "Effects of instrumental enrichment on the psychoeducational development of low-functioning adolescents." *Journal Educational Psychology.* 71(6), 751–762.

Shuy, R. 1977. *Quantitative language data: A case for and some warnings against Anthropology and Education Quarterly.* 1 (2), 78–82.

Smith, E. 1978. "The retention of the phonological, phonemic, and morphophonemic, features of Africa in Afro-American ebonies." Fullerton, Calif: Seminar Series Paper Department of Linguistics, California State University at Fullerton.

Stewart, M. 1981. "Melanin and sensori-motor intelligence." Doctoral dissertation, Georgi Peabody College of Education, Vanderbilt University.

Tryon, W. W. 1979. "The test-trait fallacy." *American Psychologist.* 4(5), 402–406.

Turner, L. D. 1969. *Africanisms in the Gullah dialect.* New York: Arnold Press.

Valentine, C. A. and B. Valentine. 1975. "Brain damage and the intellectual defense on inequality." *Current Anthropology*. March. 16(1), 117–150.

Vass, W. K. 1979. *The Bantu-speaking heritage of the United States.* Los Angeles: Center for Afro-American Studies, University of California.

Wigdor, A. K. and W. K. Garner. (Eds.). 1982. *Ability testing: Consequences and controversy.* Washington, D.C.: National Academy Press.